From Biblical Animals to Family Pets

From Biblical Animals to Family Pets

A Spiritual Evolution

MARK G. BOYER

RESOURCE *Publications* • Eugene, Oregon

FROM BIBLICAL ANIMALS TO FAMILY PETS
A Spiritual Evolution

Copyright © 2026 Mark G. Boyer. All rights reserved. Except for brief quotations in critical publications or reviews, no part of this book may be reproduced in any manner without prior written permission from the publisher. Write: Permissions, Wipf and Stock Publishers, 199 W. 8th Ave., Suite 3, Eugene, OR 97401.

Resource Publications
An Imprint of Wipf and Stock Publishers
199 W. 8th Ave., Suite 3
Eugene, OR 97401

www.wipfandstock.com

PAPERBACK ISBN: 979-8-3852-6974-7
HARDCOVER ISBN: 979-8-3852-6975-4
EBOOK ISBN: 979-8-3852-6976-1

VERSION NUMBER 031826

The scripture quotations contained herein are from the *New Revised Standard Version Updated Edition* (NRSVue), copyright © 2021 National Council of the Churches of Christ in the United States of America. Used by permission. All rights reserved worldwide.

Scripture taken from *The Message: Catholic/Ecumenical Edition* (TM), Copyright © 1993, 1994, 1995, 1996, 2000, 2001, 2002, 2013. Used by permission of NavPress Publishing Group.

Dedicated to
Henry B. and Laura D. Sivils,
neighborhood friends
and animal lovers.

. . . [E]very life is an expression of divine life.

—Rami Shapiro

. . . [C]reatures . . . share in God's perfection either simply by existing . . . or else by living and knowing particular, individual things.

—Thomas Aquinas (quoted by Bernard Piault)

Contents

Abbreviations

BB = Book of Blessings

BCE = Before the Common Era (same as BC = Before Christ)

Bibles

NRSVue = New Revised Standard Version Updated Edition
TM = The Message: Catholic/Ecumenical Edition

CB (NT) = Christian Bible (New Testament)

Acts = Acts of the Apostles
Col = Letter to the Colossians
1 Cor = First Letter of Paul to the Corinthians
2 Cor = Second Letter of Paul to the Corinthians
Heb = Letter to the Hebrews
Jude = Letter of Jude
Luke = Luke's Gospel
Mark = Mark's Gospel
Matt = Matthew's Gospel
2 Pet = Second Letter of Peter
Phil = Letter of Paul to the Philippians
Rev = Revelation
Rom = Letter of Paul to the Romans

CE = Common Era (same as AD = *Anno Domini*, in the year of the Lord)

HB (OT) = Hebrew Bible (Old Testament)

Dan = Daniel
Deut = Deuteronomy
Eccl – Ecclesiastes
Exod = Exodus
Ezek = Ezekiel

Gen = Genesis
Hos = Hosea
Isa = Isaiah
Jer = Jeremiah
Job = Job
Joel = Joel
Jonah = Jonah
Judg = Judges
1 Kgs = First Book of Kings
2 Kgs = Second Book of Kings
Lam = Lamentations
Lev = Leviticus
Mic = Micah
Num = Numbers
Prov = Proverbs
Ps(s) = Psalm(s)
1 Sam = First Book of Samuel
2 Sam = Second Book of Samuel
Zeph = Zephaniah

OT (A) = Old Testament (Apocrypha)

Bar = Baruch
2 Esd = Second Book of Esdras
Jdt = Judith
2 Macc = Second Book of Maccabees
3 Macc = Third Book of Maccabees
4 Macc = Fourth Book of Maccabees
Sg Three = Prayer of Azariah (Song of Three Jews)
Sir = Sirach (Ecclesiasticus)
Tob = Tobit
Wis = Wisdom (of Solomon)

par(s) = paragraph(s)

Punctuation Usage in Biblical Quotations

/ = indicates where one line of poetic text ends and another begins

(biblical notation) = see the specific biblical verse(s) in parentheses for more information; cf not used

– = range of verses following a colon (8:3–4)

— = range of verses from a verse in one chapter to a verse in another chapter (8:3—9:4)

a, b, c = designates first (a), second (b), third (c), etc. sentence in a verse of Scripture or a line of poetic text

Q = *Quelle*, a source shared by the authors of Matthew's Gospel and Luke's Gospel

RM = *The Roman Missal*

Introduction

TITLE: *FROM BIBLICAL ANIMALS*

This book begins with ten general reflections on animals found in the Bible. After beginning with a title and a few verses from a biblical book, a reflection follows and explores the meaning of the biblical text in context. The reflection answers the question: What did this text mean to its original audience? And what connection does this text have to other, similar references in biblical literature? Following the reflection, there is a meditation/journal question to help the reader appropriate the reflection. Basically, the question asks: How does the Scripture text connect to the reader? After spending time with the question, a psalm response, a few verses from a biblical psalm, is given to bring the exercise to a close. At the end of the chapter is found a summary of what was explored and learned in the chapter about biblical animals.

The same five-part process (title, Scripture, reflection, meditation/journal question, psalm response) is employed for the second chapter on ten biblical animal characteristics. Chapter 3 presents six exercises on biblical animal theology. Both chapters 2 and 3 conclude with a summary of what was explored and learned about biblical animals.

TITLE: *TO FAMILY PETS*

The six entries in chapter 4 are about animals as pets. The first entry is about a biblical lamb pet. And the next five entries are all about biblical dogs.

There are no references to cats in biblical literature. After a recapitulation of chapters one through four, what was learned from exploring biblical animals is applied specifically to Shelbydog, the author's deceased pet. By applying what was learned in the previous chapters, he demonstrates how his dog was a theophany, a manifestation of God, and how she nourished his spirituality. Family pets not only represent spiritual, biblical evolution, but they can help the readers who own one understand the spiritual connection they share with their pet.

The final chapter on animals and saints features thirteen saints who associated with various animals in some way, because their spirit was connected to the spirit of the animal or pet. The chapter ends with a few words on modern people, known as whisperers, who are able to connect spiritually with animals today.

SUBTITLE: *A SPIRITUAL EVOLUTION*

Biblical animals have become family pets. With the evolution from biblical animals to family pets a spiritual evolution has also occurred. The word *spiritual*, as an adjective, basically refers to aspects of one's spirit. This author prefers the word *spirit* over *soul*, because spirit is more biblical—("The LORD God formed man from the dust of the ground and breathed into his nostrils the breath [spirit] of life," Gen 2:7, NRSVue)—while soul is more philosophical, specifically Socratic, Platonic, and Aristotelian. The concept that each person possesses an immaterial and immortal soul, which is distinct from the body, did not appear in Judaism before the Babylonian exile (597 or 586 BCE to 538 BCE). In Babylon, the Jews interacted with Persian and Hellenistic philosophies. In Hebrew, the word *nephesh* is translated into English as *soul*, but it does not imply the dichotomy of its Hellenistic origin. In the Bible, the word *soul* means *living being*. When *nephesh* is translated into Greek, it becomes *psyche*. Contrary to what many people understand the word *soul* to mean, it refers to a living, breathing, conscious body. In other words, biblically, God did not make a body and put a soul into it; God, like a potter, formed a man from clay (dirt) and breathed divine breath into him, thus giving life to the man. The man became a whole creature, a soul, a living soul. Likewise, the Greek word *psyche* designates the person as a living being, a whole person. Because modern people have been philosophically programmed by Platonism and Aristotelianism, they apply the concept to an immaterial and immortal soul separate from and surviving the body to biblical texts, which do not mean what they think they do. As will be seen below, the breath of life God breathed into the man is Spirit. The

Hebrew word *ruah* (ruach) can be translated into English as breath, wind, or spirit. Thus, the man became inspirited, alive, as are all other living, breathing creatures, including animals, who were created biblically before people.

An Israelite belief illustrates this understanding. When a child is born, the child's first breath takes in the breath that the Creator has just breathed out. When the person dies and breathes his or her last breath out, the Creator breathes it in and eternal life begins. In both Hebrew and Greek, the word for breath and spirit is the same word: *ruah*, *pneuma*. Breathing is everywhere; the holy Spirit is everywhere. In other words, wherever we find living, breathing creatures, the divine Spirit is present. Thus, spirituality is the practice of awareness that each person's spirit and every animal's spirit is connected to Spirit. Each person and animal is spiritual.

The Hebrew word for breath, wind, or spirit—*ruah*— appears about four hundred times in the HB (OT) and the OT (A). Depending on the English translation, *ruah*'s first appearance in the Bible is at Genesis 1:2. *The New Revised Standard Version* (NRSV) as well as the New Revised Standard Version Updated Edition (NRSVue) states that a wind from God swept over the face of the waters, but has a footnote indicating that the phrase could also be translated as the spirit of God swept over the waters. *The Contemporary English Version* states that the Spirit of God was moving over the water. It is important to note that the NRSV and the NRSVue do not capitalize the s of spirit, but the CEV does! The immediate implication for the reader is the reference to spirit, usually understood to be the human spirit, and the reference to Spirit, usually understood to be the divine Spirit. However, in Hebrew there are no capital letters! Thus, when translators from Hebrew to English capitalize or do not capitalize the s of spirit, they are interpreting the meaning of an otherwise ambiguous text. Furthermore, translators have settled on only one meaning of the word *ruah*, which is also used for breath and wind—both human, animal, and divine!

The ambiguity associated with *ruah* does not disappear in the CB (NT). The Greek word for breath, wind, or spirit is *pneuma*. It appears nearly four hundred times. Just as in Hebrew, there are no capital letters in ancient Greek. Thus, not only is the translation of the word as breath, wind, or spirit an interpretation of the text in which it appears, but when it is translated, putting a capital S or a lowercase s on it is a further interpretation of the text. For example, in the CB (NT), the first appearance of *pneuma* in the NRSV is Matthew 1:18b: "When [Jesus'] mother Mary had been engaged to Joseph, but before they lived together, she was found to be pregnant from the Holy Spirit" (NRSVue). The phrase—"from the Holy Spirit"—could just as well be translated "from the holy breath," or "from the holy wind." The non-capitalized phrase in Greek is a descriptive title—not a name—for

God's manifestation as a spirit being or a Spirit Being. Likewise, in Mark 2:8, Jesus perceives in his spirit (*pneuma*)—where the NRSVue translators chose no capital S—but in Mark 1:10, the Spirit descends upon Jesus—where the translators chose a capital S.

In general in the NRSVue, which is used throughout this book for Scripture passages, translators of the HB (OT) and OT (A) do not use a capital S for *ruah* in any of its phrases, such as the spirit of the LORD. In the CB (NT), however, translators do use a capital S for *pneuma,* especially when the word *holy* describes it. In this book, the author uses Spirit to refer to the Divine Spirit and spirit to refer to the human or animal spirit. Because there is no way to tell how the writers of the texts intended to use either *ruah* or *pneuma*—breath, wind, or spirit—the author has chosen to let the ambiguity remain in order to plumb the richness of the spiritual benefits that exist in the biblical text. In other words, just as translators decide which meaning of the words to use in English, this author has decided to let the words mean all that they can mean in this work.

Spirit (spirit) exists in the HB (OT) and in the OT (A) before it appears in the CB (NT). However, the doctrine of the Trinity—one God, three coequal persons of Father, Son, and Holy Spirit—does not exist in the HB (OT), the OT (A), or the CB (NT). The doctrine of the Holy Spirit begins with the Ecumenical Council of Nicaea I in 325 CE and continues to develop until the end of the Ecumenical Council of Constantinople I in 381 CE. The issue known as *filioque*—referring to the Holy Spirit proceeding from the Father and the Son—was not settled until the Council of Florence in 1439 CE. Before doctrine, there was Scripture. Thus, we are exploring *ruah*—with all its meanings—in the HB (OT) and OT (A)—and *pneuma*—with all its meanings—in the CB (NT).

Biblical spirituality is the process of living one's life in relationship with whomever God is for a person. It is not about knowing biblical facts or memorized biblical verses; it is about taking such knowledge and living it daily. A person practicing biblical spirituality is not focused on convincing friends of his or her biblical truth. Biblical spirituality is living and breathing Spirit with others (spirits), especially pets, and with God (Spirit). It consists of being aware of the divine presence in other people, animals, and nature and naming it for oneself and others.

The noun *spirituality*, refers to the quality or condition of being spiritual, that is, being in touch with or aware of one's spirit connected to a pet's spirit and both connected to Spirit and nurturing it. All is in God. Known as panentheism, we already exist in the divine. Everything and everyone are in God. Everything is an expression of a dynamic process called by many names—God, Mother, Brahman, Allah, YHWH, Tao, Kali, etc. "In him we live and move," states the author of the Acts of the Apostles, "and have our being" (Acts 17:28, NRSVue). The same author explained through Jesus in Luke's Gospel that Moses "in the story about the [burning] bush," spoke of the Lord as "the God of Abraham, the God of Isaac, and the God of Jacob! Now he is God not of the dead but of the living, for to him all of them are alive" (Luke 20:37–38, NRSVue). By the time of Moses, Abraham, Isaac, and Jacob had been dead for many years. What the Lukan Jesus explains is that people and animals do not go out of existence with death, because they are alive in God throughout life, and they stay alive in God even in death. Whatever and whoever exist cannot exist outside the divine nor go out of existence. God is pure existence (being); all is spirit. All people, animals, trees, etc.—even those extinct—are alive in God. Thus, all spirituality isn't fixed, but it is fluid. God cannot be grasped and is far beyond all our ideas and words. It is best to consider God (with a capital G) to be infinite aliveness, who manifests all reality. The practice of spirituality is designed to awaken us to the biblical understanding that Spirit connects to spirit. God comes to us disguised as ourselves and as our family pets, if only we learn to pay better attention. We can access the God, who cannot be contained or even defined, anywhere, but especially in family pets. Knowing this reveals the sacredness of all inspirited life. Knowing this leads to living it. And any religion that reveals this is of great value. Today, many people think religion is broken; it is controlled by leadership that has stripped it of its spirituality and replaced it with membership, laws of belonging, commandments, and financial commitments. The flexibility religion needs to nourish spirituality is gone; the process of spirituality has ceased. It does not have a home in the modern world. People wanting spirituality get only more religion, and so they leave the churches that should be supplying spirituality. Because human beings and their pets are naturally—in terms of being in God, the source of spirit and Spirit—spiritual, nature becomes an occasion of grace. But many churches seem to have forgotten that point.

Biblical spirituality is the art of exploring nature—human and animal—to contact reality outside of words and Scripture. In reality, both human and animal being is a speck of dust, and the closer one gets to death the clearer one's understanding of life becomes. The big picture of reality presents divine life everywhere. Becoming aware of it is the goal of spirituality. Awareness is an encounter with reality; our response is not to withdraw, but to respond to the God whose Spirit moves toward our spirit through our pets. Thus, spirituality is always a process of movement: growth, development, and transformation.

Spiritual growth is about paying attention daily to areas where one may be blocked and releasing those blocks so that the energies of true self can flow. Thus, the goal of awareness (mindfulness, meditation, contemplation) is a quiet mind that gets beyond judgment and quits labeling everything as good, bad, or neutral. Spiritual practice is seeing life and it's events as they are and then deciding how to respond to them. Spirituality is how we shape our lives in response to our experience of God (Spirit) as a very real presence. We experience God, consciously or unconsciously. Once we are aware—consciously or unconsciously (intuition)—we nourish that connection in the way or ways that fill us the best. For some people, Bible reading, Bible study, other study, pottery making, dance, volunteering, cooking, caring for a pet, singing, sewing, etc. is both an experience of God (Spirit) (spirituality) and a means of nourishing personal spirituality (spirit). Divine Spirit and human spirit connect. Divine Spirit and animal spirit connect.

Knowing the essence, knowing the Divine, is knowing the universe and everyone and everything in it. If all is in God (Spirit), then all (spirits) is filled with God, and all can nourish spirituality. We pattern our lives on such sublime experiences that are brought to us by way of the ordinary. Then, we delight in them. Being in harmony with the universe is disrupted by chaos. Chaos, the daily pull to disorder or non-patterned life, keeps us out of harmony. Each person must discover and use what works for him or her to bring him or her out of chaos and back to harmony with himself or herself and with all that exists. Commonly called prayer, the practice is to reunite the broken pieces of life into a harmonious whole through reading, study, gardening, walking, painting, architecture, mountains, wildflowers, a library, a park bench, a pond, a pier, an empty ball field, a quiet museum gallery, an unused room in an office building, a hospital chapel, a lonesome tree, or the care of a pet. Divine Presence is everywhere. Spirit is everywhere and reveals itself in surprising places to the spirits of those who are aware. God (Spirit) works through each of us and through our pets to the extent to which we make ourselves receptive.

All human experience is spiritual, no matter how one limits it with descriptive adjectives, like civil, awesome, secular, religious, etc. Even though we may feel alone, we are not. We (spirits) are in God (Spirit). Spirituality is a lifetime process of stripping away the conditioning that blinds us to the truest fact of our existence: we are spirit connected to Spirit. We are immersed in God. All things are a part of God, and nothing is apart from God. Indeed, our world is in constant communication with the spiritual world. Thus, there is nothing that is not spiritual. With such awareness comes a sense of wholeness and holiness. In other words, it's an everyday acknowledgment that all (spirits) share the same divine essence (Spirit) at the core of our being. Our essential nature is infinite, eternal Spirit. That implies that there is a final eternal endpoint for human and animal existence.

While the movement of Spirit is different for different people (spirits), awareness practice teaches us to let ourselves be surprised by God. We practice spiritual awareness to be found by God, who is already present with us. Spiritual practices awaken us to the divine presence. Such disciplined activities are essential to the spiritual life; yet spiritual attainment is not the result of one's own efforts, but the result of the experience of oneness with Ultimate Reality (God). The spiritual life is not another commodity, but a discipline of awareness that leads to transformation. The individual person (spirit) journeys to the self where he or she knows all is God (Spirit). God (Spirit) works through each person (spirit) to the extent to which each makes him- or herself receptive. And on the lifetime journey, a pet may be the spirit with whom the human spirit connects to discover the presence of the Divine.

NOTES ON THE BIBLE

Three Parts

The Bible is divided into two parts: The Hebrew Bible (Old Testament) and the Christian Bible (New Testament). The Hebrew Bible consists of thirty-nine named books accepted by Jews and Protestants as Holy Scripture. The Old Testament also contains those thirty-nine books plus seven to fifteen more named books or parts of books called the Apocrypha or the Deuterocanonical Books; the Old Testament is accepted by Catholics and several other Christian denominations as Holy Scripture. The Christian Bible, consisting of twenty-seven named books, is also called the New Testament; it is accepted by Christians as Holy Scripture. Thus, in this work:

—Hebrew Bible (Old Testament), abbreviated HB (OT), indicates that a book is found both in the Hebrew Bible and the Old Testament;

—Old Testament (Apocrypha), abbreviated OT (A), indicates that a book is found only in the Old Testament Apocrypha and not in the Hebrew Bible;

—and Christian Bible (New Testament), abbreviated CB (NT), indicates that a book is found only in the Christian Bible or New Testament.

In notating biblical texts, the first number refers to the chapter in the book, and the second number (following the colon) refers to the verse within the chapter. Thus, HB (OT) Isa 7:11 means that the quotation comes from Isaiah, chapter 7, verse 11. OT (A) Sir 39:30 means that the quotation comes from Sirach, chapter 39, verse 30. CB (NT) Mark 6:2 means that the quotation comes from Mark's Gospel, chapter 6, verse 2. When more than one sentence appears in a verse, the letters a, b, c, etc. indicate the sentence being referenced in the verse. Thus, HB (OT) 2 Kgs 1:6a means that the quotation comes from the Second Book of Kings, chapter 1, verse 6, sentence 1. Also, poetry, such as the Psalms and sections of Judith, Proverbs, Isaiah, and others may be noted using the letters a, b, c, etc. to indicate the lines being used. Thus, Ps 16:4a refers to the first line of verse 4 of Psalm 16; there are two more lines of verse 4: b and c.

Because there may be a difference in the verse numbers between the *New Revised Standard Version Updated Edition* (NRSVue) and the Vulgate (the Latin translation of the Septuagint, such as *The New American Bible Revised Edition*, verse numbers may be off by a verse or two. This is true particularly with the Psalms, but with other books as well. Thus, NRSVue Isaiah 9:2–7 is NABRE (Vulgate) Isaiah 9:1–6; NRSVue Isaiah 9:2–4, 6–7 is NABRE (Vulgate) Isaiah 9:1–3, 5–6. Introductory material to Bibles usually indicates which verse-numbering is being used.

In the HB (OT) and the OT (A), the reader often sees LORD (note all capital letters). Because God's name (Yahweh or YHWH, referred to as the Tetragrammaton) is not to be pronounced, the name Adonai (meaning *Lord*) is substituted for Yahweh when a biblical text is read. When a biblical text is translated and printed, LORD (Gen 2:4) is used to alert the reader to what the text actually states: Yahweh. Furthermore, when the biblical author writes Lord Yahweh, printers present Lord GOD (note all capital letters for GOD; Gen 15:2) to avoid the printed ambiguity of LORD LORD. The Psalms in *The Message* substitute GOD (note all capital letters) for Yahweh. When the reference is to Jesus, the word printed is Lord (note capital L and lower-case letters; Luke 11:1). When writing about a lord (note all lower-case letters; Matt 18:25) with servants, no capital L is used.

In this book, *cf* (meaning *confer*) has not been used. Biblical notations placed in parentheses indicate where the reference can be found in the Bible. For example, the Second Book of Samuel records King David writing a song (2 Sam 22:1–51). The notation in parentheses is given to the reader, who may wish to look up the full reference in his or her Bible. In some instances, a few notations appear in parentheses; again, the reader may wish to see the references in their contexts.

Bibles

Most Bible readers are not aware that there is no such thing as the original Bible! The fact is: There are Bibles. First, there is the Jewish Bible, often called the Hebrew Bible; its books were collected and completed between 70 and 90 CE based on the Jerusalem canon (collection) in this order: Torah (Genesis, Exodus, Leviticus, Numbers, Deuteronomy), Prophets (Isaiah, Jeremiah, Ezekiel, etc.), and Writings (Job, Psalms, Proverbs, etc.). It is important to note the arrangement of the collected books. Second, there is—for want of a better name—the Christian Hebrew Bible, completed in the fourth century CE, but not defined until after the Reformation. It consists of Torah, Writings, and Prophets. It is important to note the (re)ordering of the collected books. Christianity took the Jewish (Hebrew) Bible and rearranged the order of its books! Then, Christianity named it the Old Testament.

The Jerusalem canon, obviously, is the collection of biblical books used in Jerusalem and its environs. A large community of Jews, however, lived in Alexandria, Egypt. To the Jerusalem canon (books in Hebrew and Aramaic) they added books in Greek, the language they spoke; this collection is the Alexandrine canon. They also translated the Jerusalem canon's books from Hebrew and Aramaic into Greek. That translation, containing books and parts of books not in the Jerusalem canon, is called the Septuagint (abbreviated LXX). Later, the Septuagint was translated into Latin; it is known as the Vulgate. Every time a book of the Bible is translated, it picks up something and it loses something; that is because there is no such thing as literary equivalence.

Thus, we have (1) the Hebrew Bible—the Jewish Bible, (2) the Hebrew Bible (Old Testament)—the rearranged books of the Hebrew Bible, and (3) the Christian Bible—twenty-seven books originally written in Greek. The Protestant Bible contains only the books in the Jerusalem canon, but rearranged into the Old Testament, plus the Christian Bible books; the Catholic Bible contains the books in the Alexandrine collection plus the Christian Bible books.

The extra books or parts of books found in the Catholic Bible (and coming from the Alexandrine collection of the Jewish Bible), but not found in a Protestant Bible, are collectively referred to as the Apocrypha or Deuterocanonical Books. They include Tobit, Judith, additions to Esther, Wisdom (of Solomon), Sirach (Ecclesiasticus), Baruch, Letter of Jeremiah, Prayer of Azariah (addition to Daniel), Susanna (addition to Daniel), Bel and the Dragon (addition to Daniel), 1 Maccabees, 2 Maccabees, 1 Esdras, Prayer of Manasseh, Psalm 151, 3 Maccabees, 2 Esdras, and 4 Maccabees. Not every Christian group, such as Catholics, accepts all the books in the Apocrypha as Scripture; for example, out of the four books of Maccabees, Catholics accept only 1 and 2 Maccabees. In Catholic Bibles, the additional books are placed with similar books. Thus, First and Second Maccabees are inserted with the historical books; the books of Wisdom and Sirach are found in the wisdom literature section.

Thus, there is no single or original Bible; there are many Bibles; it depends on what books a specific denomination or group (Jews, Christians) accepts as Scripture. The Bible that contains any book that any group accepts as Scripture is *The Access Bible* (updated edition): *New Revised Standard Version with the Apocrypha*, general editors Gail R. O'Day and David Petersen, published in New York by Oxford University Press in 1999 and updated in 2011. In 2021, the NRSV was published by Zondervan as the New Revised Standard Version updated edition (NRSVue), which, like its predecessor, contains all the books any group of people may consider to be a part of their Bible.

Thus, a Bible reader should keep in mind the following: In a Christian Bible, The Old Testament consists of the rearranged books found in the Hebrew (Jewish) Bible. Roman Catholics and some others add some books and parts of books to that Old Testament because they were found in the Alexandrine collection. In general, Protestants do not add books to the Old Testament; they follow the Jerusalem collection of books, but rearrange them as noted above. Almost all Christians accept the twenty-seven books of the New Testament; there are a few groups who reject one or another of the books in the collection.

Thus, as you can see, this can become difficult to navigate, especially when someone says, "The Bible says . . . ." The astute Bible reader needs to ask, "Which book in which Bible says that?" There is no such thing as the original Bible. There are Bibles, various libraries of books collected over three thousand years by individuals and groups who declared their collection (canon) to be Scripture. When engaged in Bible study, it is also important to note that the Bible is a library of books written by different authors at different times in history; it is not a single book. While the authors of various books often agree with each other, there are occasions when they disagree with each other.

Presuppositions

The HB (OT) begins as stories passed on by word of mouth from one person to another. Sometime during the oral transmission stage, authors decided to collect the oral stories and write them. A change occurs immediately. One does not tell a story the same way one writes a story. Repetition and correction occur in oral story-telling. Except for future emendations by copyists, single statements by characters and plot structure dominate written stories. Furthermore, in both oral and written story-telling, types or models are employed. In the HB (OT), for example, Joshua and Elijah are types of Moses.

In the CB (NT) Elizabeth becomes a type of Hannah, who is herself a type of Sarah. When orally narrating or writing a story, the teller or author consciously creates one character as a type of another to make the character and his or her words and actions intelligible to the hearer or reader.

In the CB (NT) the oldest gospel is Mark's account of Jesus' victory. The author of Matthew's Gospel copied and shortened about eighty percent of Mark's material into his book and then added other stories to make the work longer. The author of Luke's Gospel copied and shortened about fifty percent of Mark's material into his orderly account and then added other stories to make the work much longer. The material shared by Matthew and Luke is called Q—from the German word *Quelle*, meaning *Source*—by biblical scholars. Mark's Gospel begins as oral story-telling, lasting for about forty years in that form. An unidentified author, called Mark for the sake of convenience, collects the oral stories, sets a plot, and writes the first gospel around 70 CE. Because Jesus was expected to return soon, no one had thought about recording what he had said and done until Mark came along and realized that he was not returning as quickly as had been thought. About ten years after Mark finished his gospel, Matthew needed to adopt Mark's narrative—originally intended for a peasant gentile readership—to a Jewish audience. And about twenty years after Mark finished his gospel, Luke needed to adapt Mark's poor gentile-intended work for a rich, upper class, urban, gentile readership. The author of John's Gospel did not know the existence of the other three works collectively named synoptic gospels. A point often overlooked by modern readers is the fact that they are not the intended readers of biblical texts. Every biblical book was written to a specific group of people at a specific time in history. Thus, Paul did not write to people living in the United States; he wrote in Greek to people living in Rome, Corinth, and Thessalonica. Modern readers are reading an English translation (and interpretation) with Roman-Greco cultural presuppositions underlying the text.

Furthermore, letters and gospels were not first intended to be read privately as is done today. They were meant to be heard in a group. The very low rate of literacy in the first century would have never dictated many copies of texts since most people could not read, and their standard practice was to listen to another read the letters and stories to them. Thus, what began as oral story-telling passed on by word of mouth became written story-telling preserved in gospels. A careful reading of Mark's Gospel will reveal the orality still embedded in the text, especially evident in the repetition of words and the organization of stories in three parts. In rewriting Mark, Matthew and Luke removed the last traces of oral story-telling.

The letters of Paul are older than the gospels. Biblical scholars divide the letters of Paul into the authentic letters—those written by Paul (Romans, Galatians, Philippians, etc.)—and those written by someone else in Paul's name—second generation Pauline letters (Ephesians, Colossians, Titus, etc.). The latter group of letters usually develop Pauline thought for a new generation of Christians. The reader of letters needs to keep in mind that the letter was not addressed to him or her; it was addressed to a specific group of believers in the mid- to late-first century CE. In addition to the Pauline body of letters, there are other letters that were gathered and placed in the CB (NT) canon (collection), such as James, 1 and 2 Peter, Jude, etc. These anonymous letters were written in the name of an apostle to give them authority in the Christian communities to which they were addressed.

Furthermore, it is important to understand that there are three different Pauls presented in the CB (NT). There is the Acts of the Apostles Paul, who is presented by the same author who wrote Luke's Gospel; in other words, Luke-Acts is a two-volume work. There is original Paul, the man who wrote or dictated letters attributed to him. And there is second-generation Paul, others who wrote under Paul's name to update some of original Paul's ideas for the next generation of believers. The caution here is to be sure that a reader is not interpreting original Paul through the lens of the Acts of the Apostles Paul. While all three Pauls are similar, their theological positions are quite different.

1

Biblical Animals

IN GENERAL

. . . God . . . , you, . . . the source of life, / have made all that is, / so that you might fill your creatures with blessings . . . .[1]

Living Creatures

Scripture: ". . . God said, 'Let the earth bring forth living creatures of every kind: cattle and creeping things and wild animals of the earth of every kind.' And it was so." (Gen 1:24, NRSVue)

Reflection: The author of the first story of creation (the younger of the two with which the HB [OT] book of Genesis begins), known as the Priestly

1. "Order," RM, par 116.

Source, classifies cattle, insects, and wild animals as living creatures. All of these are land animals, distinguished from the living creatures of the waters and birds of the sky (Gen 1:20–23). The specific mention of cattle indicates that even before biblical times cows had been domesticated. Besides plowing fields, threshing, and pulling carts, cattle provided milk, meat, and sacrifices. Because they were considered property, they indicated wealth. Creeping things are insects, like bees, ants, locusts, flies, crickets, beetles, and grasshoppers. The wild animals of the earth include lions, leopards, bears, and wolves, which evoked fear in people. The wild animals are not domesticated animals. Thus, land animals are clearly distinguished from everything created before them; they are living creatures, occupying a higher status than the plants, but a rung below humans, who have dominion over the fish, the birds, the cattle, every creeping thing, and all the wild animals of the earth (Gen 1:26). Other biblical authors mention the animals of the earth (Job 35:11; Isa 18:6; Jer 7:33, and Ezek 29:5)—also referred to as animals of the field (Ezek 31:6; Dan 2:38, 4:12, 21, 23, 32; Joel 2:22; and 2 Esd 7:65) and animals of the land (Ezek 3:25, 28; and 38:20). The animals of the earth, as creatures, are an extension of God, their creator, sharing divine life in various degrees, and, as such, deserve to be treated with respect regardless of their level of consciousness and intelligence.

Meditation/Journal: In your experience, which animal of the earth deserves respect, because it is a living a creature of the Creator?

Psalm Response: "Mountain goats climb about the cliffs; / badgers burrow among the rocks. / When it's dark and night takes over, / all the forest creatures come out. / The young lions roar for their prey, / clamoring to God for their supper. / When the sun comes up, they vanish, / lazily stretched out in their dens. / Oh, look—the deep, wide sea, / brimming with fish past counting, / sardines and sharks and salmon." (Ps 104:18, 20–22, 25, TM)

Breath of Life

Scripture: ". . . Noah with his sons . . . and Noah's wife and the three wives of his sons entered the ark, they and every wild animal of every kind and all domestic animals of every kind and every creeping thing that creeps on the earth and every bird of every kind. They went into the ark with Noah, two and two of all flesh in which there was the breath of life." (Gen 7:13–15, NRSVue)

Reflection: While the biblical narrative concerning Noah, the ark, and the saving of animals from an imminent flood represents the melding of the two different flood stories—the Yahwist and the Priestly—the Scripture passage above is from the Priestly Source. For example, the Priestly story states that Noah was to bring two of every kind of animal into the ark (Gen 6:19), while the Yahwist account specifies seven pairs of clean animals and birds and one pair of unclean animals (Gen 7:2–3). No matter the number of animals, all of them contain the breath of life, breathed into them by the LORD God. Like a potter at his wheel, the LORD God created people from clay and breathed into their nostrils the breath of life, and they became living beings (Gen 2:7). The biblical author maintains that the LORD in creating animals filled them with the breath of life, too. Indeed, God tells Noah that he intends to destroy with the flood all flesh in which is the breath of life (Gen 7:17). Later, the biblical author states that "everything on dry land in whose nostrils was the breath of life died" (Gen 7:22, NRSVue). The reference is not just to the physical act of respiration, but implies a spiritual animating force, a life-force, energy, spirit that flows through all living beings. The force cannot be seen, but can be experienced. Some people name it soul, but, because of Aristotelian and Platonic philosophy's dichotomy between body and soul, the unity of flesh and spirit is lost. No matter by what name it is called, its purpose is to highlight that God is the ultimate source of life and the intimate connection between creation and the Creator. In other words, the breath of life signifies a spiritual reality connecting animals and people to God.

Meditation/Journal: What word do you use to describe the spiritual connection that exists between animals, people, and God? What are the positive and negative limitations of your word?

Psalm Response: "What a wildly wonderful world, GOD! / You made it all, with Wisdom at your side, / made earth overflow with your wonderful creations. / All the creatures look expectantly to you / to give them their meals on time. / You come, and they gather around; / you open your hand and they eat from it. / If you turned your back, / they'd die in a minute— / Take back your Spirit and they die, / revert to original mud; / Send out your Spirit and they spring to life . . . ." (Ps 104:24, 27–30a, TM)

Wild Animals

Scripture: ". . . God remembered Noah and all the wild animals . . . that were with him in the ark. And God made a wind blow over the earth, and the waters subsided . . . ." (Gen 8:1, NRSVue)

Reflection: As already noted above, according to the author of the HB (OT) book of Genesis, God created wild animals, which Noah took with him in the ark to protect them from the waters of the great flood. In due time, as the story unfolds, God remembers Noah, the ark, and the wild animals, and prepares to re-create the world. Animals, such as the lion, bear, and wolf, represent wildness; wild animals are free from most human interference and are known, usually, as being dangerous to humankind. The mere mention of wild animals elicits fear in people. However, God has them under his divine control. Thus, every seventh year, when the land is supposed to lie fallow, after the poor have gathered what it produced on its own, what the poor leave behind the wild animals may eat (Exod 23:11a). However, God also promises to keep in check the populations of wild animals, when the Israelites enter Canaan (Exod 23:29), but, if need be, he may use them to discipline the people's disobedience (Lev 26:22). The author of the HB (OT) book of Job mentions wild animals (Job 5:22–23; 28:8), especially those who play in the mountains (Job 40:20). According to the HB (OT) book of Proverbs, the lion is the mightiest among wild animals (Prov 30:30). The prophet Isaiah depicts the destruction of Babylon as being the place where wild animals gather to rest (Isa 13:21). After Babylon is destroyed, the LORD declares that the wild animals will honor him (Isa 43:20) by doing his bidding (Isa 56:9). The prophet Jeremiah states that the bodies of the dead will become food for wild animals (Jer 16:4; 19:7), while the prophet Ezekiel sees wild animals ravage Jerusalem (Ezek 14:15, 21). During a time of devastation, the prophet Joel writes that the wild animals cry to the LORD (Joel 1:20), while the prophet Zephaniah declares that a desolate city becomes the lair for wild animals (Zeph 2:15). Thus, in biblical literature, wild animals represent that part of creation that is not under the control of humankind; only God can control wild animals.

Meditation/Journal: What wild animal is your favorite? What does that wild animal represent to you? Explain.

Psalm Response: "Praise GOD from earth, / you sea dragons, you fathomless ocean deeps . . . . / Wild beasts and herds of cattle, / snakes, and birds in flight . . . . / Let them praise the name of God— / it's the only Name worth praising." (Ps 148:7, 10, 13, TM)

Domestic Animals

Scripture: ". . . God said to Noah and to his sons with him, 'As for me, I am establishing my covenant with you and your descendants after you and with every living creature that is with you, the birds, the domestic animals, and every animal of the earth with you, as many as came out of the ark.'" (Gen 9:8–10, NRSVue)

Reflection: Only in the narrative about the great flood is there found a reference to domestic animals in biblical literature. The HB (OT) book of Genesis contains the flood narrative from 6:1 to 9:28, even though, as already mentioned, two different versions of the story have been melded into one. Domestic animals (Gen 7:14, 21; 8:1; 9:10—above), as already mentioned above, include cattle, sheep, goats, camels, donkeys, mules, and horses. Usually referred to as tame animals, they were kept because they served multiple purposes. For example, cattle provided milk, cheese, meat, and clothing. Sheep provided wool for clothes, meat, and sacrifices. Goats gave milk, meat, and sacrifices. Camels, donkeys, mules, and horses, besides providing transportation, also helped farmers in their fields. Humankind's relationship to domestic animals was a parallel to God's relationship to humankind. Just like people knew the needs of their domestic animals, so God knew the needs of people (Prov 12:10). Because of the abundance of domestic animals, they are seldom mentioned in biblical literature; in other words, they are taken for granted.

Meditation/Journal: What domestic animal is your favorite? What does that domestic animal represent to you? Explain.

Psalm Response: "Sing to GOD a thanksgiving hymn, / play music on your instruments to God, / Who fills the sky with clouds, / preparing rain for the earth, / Then turning the mountains green with grass, / feeding both cattle and crows. / He's not impressed with horsepower; / the size of our muscles means little to him. / Those who fear GOD get GOD's attention; / they can depend on his strength." (Ps 147:7–11, TM)

Sign Animals

Scripture: "The wolf shall live with the lamb; / the leopard shall lie down with the kid; / the calf and the lion will feed together, / and a little child shall lead them. / The cow and the bear shall graze; / their young shall lie down together; / and the lion shall eat straw like the ox. / The nursing child shall play over the hole of the asp, / and the weaned child shall put its hand on the adder's den." (Isa 11:6–8, NRSVue)

Reflection: A sign is a thing that points to another thing. For example, a specific flag points to a specific country or state or city. The red octagon posted on a pole points a driver to STOP, even if the word is not printed in white on the red sign. When imagining a time of world peace, the First Prophet Isaiah pairs wild and domestic animals—enemies of each other—as living in harmony with each other, the way that nations should exist together. Wolves eat lambs, except in Isaiah. Leopards eat baby goats, except in Isaiah. Calves and lions do not eat the same food, except in Isaiah. Bears eat grazing cows; they do not graze side-by-side, except in Isaiah. Lions and oxen do not eat straw together; lions prefer red meat, while oxen prefer straw—except in Isaiah. According to the prophetic sign, however, an end will come to violence and disorder of God's world; harmony, signified by animals who are usually enemies of each other, would result from a new heaven and a new earth (Isa 65:25; 66:2–3).

Meditation/Journal: Where do you see animals as signs of world harmony, peace, and unity.

Psalm Response: "After Israel left Egypt, / the clan of Jacob left those barbarians behind; / Judah became holy land for him, / Israel the place of holy rule. / The mountains turned playful and skipped like rams, / the hills frolicked like spring lambs. / And mountains, why did you skip like rams? / and you, hills, frolic like spring lambs? / Tremble, Earth! You're in the Lord's presence! / in the presence of Jacob's God." (Ps 114:1–2, 4, 6–7, TM)

Clean and Unclean Animals

Scripture: "Of clean animals and of animals that are not clean and of birds and of everything that creeps on the ground, two and two, male and female, went into the ark with Noah, as God had commanded Noah." (Gen 7:8–9, NRSVue)

Reflection: The mention of clean and unclean animals this early in the HB (OT) book of Genesis indicates that the narrative about Noah, the ark, and the animals came into existence after the dietary laws had been established later in Israelite history. Clean and unclean do not refer to physical dirt or grime or the lack thereof. The designation of animals being clean or unclean involves a whole dietary system. Any animal possessing two or more characteristics that usually go together is considered clean. For example, in general ocean creatures have scales and fins. However, there are other ocean creatures that do no have scales and fins, such as clams or oysters, and they are considered to be unclean. The HB (OT) book of Leviticus (11:1–47) and Deuteronomy (14:3–21) present lists of animals that are clean and unclean. Leviticus 11:1–8 is focused on land animals possessing divided hooves, cleft-feet, and chewing the cud. If a land animal possesses all three characteristics, such as cattle, sheep, and some wild game, it was considered clean and could be eaten. However, because one or more characteristics were missing, camels, rabbits, and pigs were considered unclean and could not be eaten. While the distinctions may seem arbitrary to modern people, they provided a means for Israelites and Jews to establish dietary regulations, which became known as kosher.

Meditation/Journal: In your culture, what animals are considered to be clean, that is, able to be eaten? What animals are considered to be unclean, that is, not able to be eaten?

Canticle Response: "Water mammals and fish, bless the Lord; praise and honor him forever. / All creatures that fly, bless the Lord; praise and honor him forever. / All beasts tame and wild, bless the Lord; praise and honor him forever. / All the offspring of the world, bless the Lord; praise and honor him forever." (Dan 3:79–82 [Sg Three 1:57–60], NRSVue)

Blood: Life

Scripture: "God blessed Noah and his sons and said to them, . . . 'The fear and dread of you shall rest on every animal of the earth and on every bird of the air, on everything that creeps on the ground and on all the fish of the sea; into your hand they are delivered. . . . [Y]ou shall not eat flesh with its life, that is, its blood. . . . [F]rom every animal I will require it . . . .'" (Gen 9:1–2. 4–5, NRSVue)

Reflection: In biblical understanding, the blood of a clean animal being slaughtered to eat must have its blood drained from its flesh. Blood represents life, which must be returned to God; thus, the blood of an animal slaughtered for food is collected and poured into the earth. That is why after Cain kills Abel, the LORD tells Cain, ". . . [Y]our brother's blood is crying out to me from the ground!" (Gen 4:10b, NRSVue). As noted, the above passage in Genesis was written long after the prohibition concerning blood had been instituted. In the HB (OT) book of Deuteronomy, Moses is depicted telling the Israelites, ". . . [B]e sure that you do not eat the blood; for the blood is the life, and you shall not eat the life with the meat. Do not eat it; you shall pour it out on the ground like water" (Deut 12:23–24, NRSVue). What had been a vegetarian diet (Gen 1:29–30) became a carnivorous diet. People rule the land animals; the animals must fear their rulers, because they can be killed for food. Once altars come into existence, the blood of animals is dashed against the altar (Lev 17:6). ". . . [T]he life of the flesh is in the blood," states God, "and I have given it to you for making atonement

. . . , for, as life, it is the blood that makes atonement" (Lev 17:11). Even in modern times, the sight of blood leads to the conclusion that life is flowing from a person, while giving blood is giving life.

Meditation/Journal: When you see blood, what do you conclude?

Psalm Response: "This is God, your God, / speaking to you. / I don't find fault with your acts of worship, / the frequent burnt sacrifices you offer. But why should I want your blue-ribbon bull, / or more and more goats from your herds? / Every creature in the forest is mine, / the wild animals on all the mountains. / Do you think I feast on venison? / or drink draughts of goat's blood? / Spread for me a banquet of praise, / serve High God a feast of kept promises . . . ." (Ps 50:7–10, 13–14, TM)

Firstborn

Scripture: "The LORD said to Moses, 'Consecrate to me all the firstborn; whatever is the first to open the womb among . . . animals is mine.' Moses said to the people . . . , 'All the firstborn offspring of your livestock that are males shall be the LORD's.'" (Exod 13:1–2, 3a, 12b, NRSVue)

Reflection: The HB (OT) book of Leviticus states clearly, "A firstling of animals . . . , which as a firstling belongs to the LORD, cannot be consecrated by anyone [to the LORD] whether ox or sheep, it is the LORD's" (Lev 27:26, NRSVue). Also, the HB (OT) book of Numbers records the LORD telling Aaron, ". . . [T]he firstborn of a cow or the firstborn of a sheep or the firstborn of a goat . . . [is] holy. You shall dash their blood on the altar . . ." (Num 18:17, NRSVue). The author of the HB (OT) book of Exodus explains why the firstborn of animals belongs to the LORD. The Pharaoh of Egypt refused to let the Hebrews leave his country. However, his stubbornness was overcome when the LORD killed the firstborn of animals. Thus, the Israelites are instructed to sacrifice to the LORD every male that first opens the womb in remembrance of what God did for them (Exod 13:14–16). It was by the LORD's strength that the Hebrews left Egypt.

Meditation/Journal: Today, what is like the firstborn belonging to the LORD in Israelite culture? Explain.

Psalm Response: "I . . . give witness to the greatness of GOD, / our Lord, high above all other gods. / He does just as he pleases— / however, wherever, whenever. / He struck down the Egyptian firstborn, . . . animal firstborn. / He made Egypt sit up and take notice, / confronted Pharaoh and his servants with miracles." (Ps 135:5–6, 8–9, TM)

Corpses for Wild Animals

Scripture: "Thus says the LORD: All you wild animals, / all you wild animals in the forest, come to devour!" (Isa 56:1a, 9, NRSVue)

Reflection: The LORD's call to wild animals to come to devour the corpses of his people is, in fact, a summons to foreign nations to come and punish his people. According to Isaiah, the LORD declares, "The wild animals will honor me" (Isa 43:20a); in other words, the foreign nations will honor the LORD, while his own people fail to do so. This idea is best expressed by the prophet Micah, who provides the only other biblical reference to animals in the forest: ". . . [A]mong the nations the remnant of Jacob, / surrounded by many peoples, / shall be like a lion among the animals of the forest, / like a young lion among the flocks of sheep, / which, when it goes through, treads down / and tears in pieces, with no one to deliver" (Mic 5:8, NRSVue). Both the prophets Jeremiah and Ezekiel exploit the imagery of the corpses of the LORD's own people being food for wild animals, sometimes referred to as animals of the earth (Jer 7:33, 12:9, 16:4, 19:7, 34:20; Ezek 32:4, 33:27, 34:5, 8). The idea is also found in the HB (OT) prophet Hosea (2:12) in the OT (A) Second Book of Maccabees (9:15) and in the Third Book of Maccabees (6:7). While the image of wild animals devouring people (Isa 18:6; Ezek 29:5) disturbs modern humans, the biblical depiction is designed to show that the LORD is in charge of everything that takes places on the earth he created.

Meditation/Journal: What are your feelings about the LORD summoning wild animals to devour errant people?

Psalm Response: "God! Barbarians have broken into your home, / violated your holy temple, / left Jerusalem a pile of rubble! / They've served up the corpses of your servants / as carrion food for birds of prey, / Threw the bones of your holy people / out to the wild animals to gnaw on. / They dumped out their blood / like buckets of water. / All around Jerusalem, their bodies / were left to rot, unburied. / We're nothing but a joke to our neighbors, / graffiti scrawled on the city walls." (Ps 79:1–4, TM)

Animal Rest

Scripture: ". . . God spoke all these words, 'Remember the Sabbath day and keep it holy. Six days you shall labor and do all your work. But the seventh day is a Sabbath to the LORD your God; you shall not do any work—you, . . . or . . . your livestock . . . .'" Exod 20:1, 8–10, NRSVue)

Reflection: According to the commandment found in the HB (OT) book of Exodus, the LORD tells Moses that both people and their livestock are to observe the Sabbath rest by doing no work. The reason given is that just as the LORD took six days to create heaven and earth and rested on the seventh day, people and animals should rest on the seventh day (Exod 20:11). The writer observes that the LORD blessed the seventh or Sabbath day and consecrated it (Exod 20:11). This commandment puts animals—here mentioned as livestock—on the same level. In the HB (OT) book of Deuteronomy, the same commandment is more specific. Not only are people to do no work on the Sabbath, but neither are their ox, donkey, or any livestock (Deut 5:14). In this book more animals are set beside people equally. Oxen, donkeys, livestock, and people together observe the Sabbath rest, commanded by God (Deut 5:15). While it was not the Sabbath (Saturday) that was observed rigorously in the past, it was Sunday that was kept as a day of rest. Businesses were closed, offices were closed, banks were closed, but over the course of time the blue laws, which dictated such closures, were removed, and the result was almost everything was kept open on Sunday just like it was the previous six days.

Meditation/Journal: How do you observe the Sabbath (Saturday) or Sunday? Why? In what specific ways do your pets participate in your observance(s)?

Psalm Response: "All creation, bless the Lord; praise and honor him forever. / Water mammals and fish, bless the Lord; praise and honor him forever. / All creatures that fly, bless the Lord; praise and honor him forever. / All beasts tame and wild, bless the Lord; praise and honor him forever. / Stand up and proclaim the greatness of the Lord; he is goodness itself and his mercy never quits." (Dan 3:57, 79–81, 89 [Sg Three 1:34, 56–58, 66], TM).

Summary

Biblically, God created animals—of the earth, land, and field—both wild and domestic as living creatures endowed with divine life in some measure. Thus, animals—both wild and domestic—are extensions of God. All animals possess the breath of life, according to biblical authors. After the great flood, God establishes a covenant with the animals which came out of the ark; he pledges never to flood the earth again. Then, for dietary purposes animals are divided into categories of clean and unclean. Noah and his descendants are established by God as masters of all the animals; they can kill and eat those determined to be clean, but they are not permitted to eat their blood, because, like the breath of life, the blood indicates divine life in animals. Because blood, life, divine life belongs to God, the blood of animals must be poured into the earth or dashed upon an altar from which it runs into the earth to indicate that the blessing of animals, the life, the blood, the breath comes from God and returns to God. As such, the first-born of animals, especially the male, belongs to God; it is to be sacrificed as a remembrance of the death of the firstborn, which precipitated the escape of the Hebrews from Egyptian slavery. Because of their disobedience, especially their idolatry, the Lord through the prophets promise the Israelites that some of them (along with others) will be killed and their corpses will be food for wild animals. Because animals observe the Sabbath rest, they are on equal footing with people, who rest on the seventh day of the week in imitation of the LORD (God), who, after creating for six days, rested on the seventh day.

2

Animal Characteristics

UNDER GOD'S CONTROL

The animals of God's creation . . . share in the fortunes of human existence and have a part in human life. God, who confers his gifts on all living things, has often used the service of animals or made them symbolic reminders of the gifts of salvation.[1]

Covenant

Scripture: "On that day, says the LORD, . . . I will make for you a covenant . . . with the wild animals, the birds of the air, and the creeping things of the ground, and I will abolish the bow, the sword, and war from the land, I will make you lie down in safety." (Hos 2:16a, 18, NRSVue)

Reflection: While animals are ruled by humans (Gen 1:26; Bar 3:16), they serve as intermediaries for the LORD, who often, biblically, takes control of them himself. This is what the HB (OT) prophet Hosea depicts taking place. Already in the HB (OT) book of Genesis, God had established a covenant with Noah and with every living creature (Gen 9:9–10). Just as God saved Noah, his descendants, and animals, through the prophet Hosea, he promises to do it again. Humankind and animal-kind are partners in the same covenant with God. That covenant, as it did with Noah, will result in divine order and peace in the natural world, and it will be based on righteousness,

1. "Blessing," BB, par 949.

justice, steadfast love, mercy, and faithfulness. The LORD brings those qualities to the covenant relationship, and he expects animals (and people) to reciprocate. In a similar way, after Jerusalem and Judah are defeated and destroyed by the Babylonians, the prophet Jeremiah records: "Thus says the LORD: In this place of which you [captives] say, 'It is a waste without humans or animals,' in the towns of Judah and the streets of Jerusalem that are desolate, without inhabitants, human or animal, there shall once more be heard . . . the voices of those who sing as they bring thank offerings to the house of the LORD . . ." (Jer 33:10–11, NRSVue). Then, Jeremiah adds, "Thus says the LORD of hosts: In this place that is waste, without humans or animals, and in all its towns there shall again be pasture for shepherds resting their flocks" (Jer 33:12, NRSVue). In other words, the LORD considers animals to be worthy partners in his covenant.

Meditation/Journal: In what specific ways do you see animals as partners in covenant with God?

Psalm Response: "Hallelujah! / I give thanks to GOD with everything I've got— / This GOD of Grace, this GOD of Love. / He remembered to keep his ancient promise. / He proved to his people that he could do what he said . . . . / He ordered his Covenant kept forever." (Ps 111:1a, 3, 6a, 8, TM)

Holiness

Scripture: The LORD said to Moses, "You shall set limits for the people all around, saying, 'Be careful not to go up the mountain or to touch the edge of it. Any who touch the mountain shall be put to death. No hand shall touch them, but they shall be stoned or shot with arrows; whether animal or human being they shall not live.'" (Exod 19:12–13a, NRSVue)

Reflection: After the Israelites have escaped Egyptian slavery, they travel to Mount Sinai (Horeb), where Moses had first encountered the LORD in a burning bush that was not consumed (Exod 3:1—4:17). After Moses climbs the mountain and gets directions from the LORD, he descends and delivers God's words. As noted in the biblical passage above, the people are informed that the LORD will come to Mount Sinai (Horeb), and there will be limits as to how far the people and animals can get to the mountain. It is important to note here that the animals possess a dignity that is either a little lesser than or equal to the Israelites. If the holy mountain is touched, according to the HB (OT) text, whoever touches it is to be stoned or shot full of arrows! No matter what punishment is chosen, the results are the same: death. In the CB (NT), the author of the Letter to the Hebrews informs his readers that they have not come to a mountain, like the Israelites of old, who "could not endure the order that was given, 'If even an animal touches the mountain, it shall be stoned to death'" (Heb 12:20). Instead, Hebrews' readers have reached the city of the living God (Heb 12:22). The prohibition not to touch the mountain in Genesis is based on the definition of holiness, which means to set apart from immorality, sin, and the profane. Because the LORD is absolutely, morally pure and perfect, both people and animals must not only be likewise separated from others and dedicated to him, but set apart from all else as his.

Meditation/Journal: What do you understand biblical holiness to mean? How might you explain it to another?

Psalm Response: "GOD rules. On your toes, everybody! / He towers in splendor over all the big names. / Great and terrible your beauty; let everyone praise you! / Holy. Yes, holy. / Lift high GOD, our God; worship at his holy mountain. / Holy. Yes, holy is GOD our God." (Ps 99:1a, 3, 9, TM)

Four-Footed Animals

Scripture: ". . . What can be known about God is plain to [to the gentiles], because God has made it plain to them. Ever since the creation of the world God's eternal power and divine nature, invisible though they are, have been seen and understood through the things God has made. . . . [T]hey exchanged the glory of the immortal God for images resembling a mortal human or birds or four-footed animals or reptiles." (Rom 1:19–20a, 23, NRSVue)

Reflection: In genuine Pauline thought, the author of the CB (NT) Letter to the Romans states that God's eternal power and divine nature—even though they are invisible—can be known by examining creation. In other words, everything God created reveals God in some way. In a Pauline general sense, gentiles (non-Jews) didn't choose to see the glory of the immortal God revealed in creation, but they chose four-footed animals, like cattle; they chose to worship the creature (idolatry) instead of the Creator. In the CB (NT) Acts of the Apostles, Peter narrates a vision: "There was something like a large sheet coming down from heaven, being lowered by its four corners, and it came close to me. As I looked at it closely I saw four-footed animals, beasts of prey, reptiles, and birds of the air. I also heard a voice saying to me, 'Get up, Peter; kill and eat.' But I replied, 'By no means, Lord; for nothing profane or unclean has ever entered my mouth.' But a second time the voice answered from heaven, 'What God has made clean, you must not call profane.' This happened three times; then everything was pulled up again to heaven" (Acts 11:5b–10, NRSVue). In the Jewish world of the first century CE, gentiles were considered by Jews to be unclean. Eating with gentiles risked mixing Jewish clean and gentile unclean food, such as meat sacrificed to idols. What Peter learns from his vision is that the categories of separation established by people are not, necessarily, those established by God, who gives even to gentiles the repentance that leads to life (Acts 11:18b). Both of these accounts emphasize that four-footed animals can reveal the Creator and his acceptance of what humans consider to be impure.

Meditation/Journal: In your experience, what four-footed animal, considered unclean by you, is considered clean by others? In your experience, what four-footed animal, considered clean by you, is considered unclean by others?

Canticle Response: "All creation, bless the Lord; praise and honor him forever. / Everything above creation, bless the Lord; praise and honor him forever. / Every virtuous being, bless the Lord; praise and honor him forever. / All the earth, bless the Lord; praise and honor him forever. / All beasts tame and wild, bless the Lord; praise and honor him forever." (Dan 3:57–58, 61, 74, 81 [Sg Three 1:35–36, 39, 52, 59], TM)

Repentant Animals

Scripture: "By the decree of the king [of Nineveh] and his nobles: No human or animal, no herd or flock, shall taste anything. They shall not feed, nor shall they drink water. Humans and animals shall be covered with sackcloth, and they shall cry mightily to God." (Jonah 3:7–8a, NRSVue)

Reflection: The prophet Jonah is reluctant to go to Nineveh, so he attempts to skip the LORD's call by sailing away. However, God never takes no for an answer! Thus, after Jonah is swallowed by a large fish which deposited him on dry land, God calls again. It is important to pay attention to facts underlying the story. First, while Jonah attempts to avoid the LORD's call, the large fish hears it and heeds it! Next, Jonah is an Israelite prophet sent to preach repentance to the citizens of Nineveh, the capital of Assyria, Israel's enemy! While it takes three days to walk through Nineveh, Jonah's one-day walking and preaching are effective, as demonstrated by the Ninevites proclaiming a fast and putting on sackcloth (Jonah 3:5). If only the Israelites would have responded as quickly to the words of the prophets God sent them, they would not have been defeated by the Assyrians in 722 BCE nor the Babylonians in 586/587 BCE! When the king of Nineveh gets word of Jonah's preaching, he issues the decree found in the above Scripture text. Both people and animals fast and put on sackcloth, a rough fabric woven from hair and dark in color, worn as a sign of repentance. The modern equivalent to the biblical sackcloth would be burlap. The king's proclamation is heeded; both people and animals repent. And, the very thing the LORD wanted—the repentance of the Ninevites—is what God does through Jonah (Jonah 3:10)! Of course, Jonah is not pleased with his success, so he sulks for a short time (Jonah 4:1–10). However, the LORD, who is concerned about all people and all animals asks him, "Should I not be concerned about Nineveh, that great city, in which there are more than a hundred and twenty thousand persons who do not know their right hand from their left and also many animals?" (Jonah 4:11, NRSVue). The reader is left to answer God's question.

Meditation/Journal: How do you answer the LORD's question to Jonah? What are the consequences of the answer you give? Explain.

Prayer Response: "GOD! I knew it—when I was back home, I knew this was going to happen! That's why I ran off . . . ! I knew you were sheer grace and mercy, not easily angered, rich in love, and ready at the drop of a hat to turn your plans of punishment into a program of forgiveness. So, GOD, if you won't kill [the Ninevites], kill *me*! I'm better off dead!" (Jonah 4:1–3, TM)

Animals Teach

Scripture: ". . . [A]sk the animals, and they will teach you, / the birds of the air, and they will tell you; / ask the plants of the earth, and they will teach you, / and the fish of the sea will declare to you. / Who among all these does not know / that the hand of the LORD has done this? / In his hand is the life of every living thing / and the breath of every human being." (Job 12:7–10, NRSVue)

Reflection: After Job's friend, Zophar, has accused him of malice in maintaining his innocence, Job denounces him for trying to speak for God, who is in charge of the world he created. That is why Job urges him to learn what the animals teach: nothing happens without God. The life of every living animal is in God's hand! While Job's point is right on target, later in the book Elihu, a new character who suddenly appears in the book at the beginning of chapter 32, states that God "teaches us more than the animals of the earth / and makes us wiser than the birds of the air" (Job 35:11). In other words, according to Elihu, humankind ranks above animals, because people are taught more than the animals of the earth. There is also the reference in the above passage to the life of every living thing being in God's hand. Later in the book, Elihu will add: "If [God] should take back his spirit to himself, and gather to himself his breath, / all flesh would perish together, / and all mortals return to dust" (Job 34:14–15, NRSVue). According to Elihu, animals, like people, were made by the spirit of God, "and the breath of the Almighty gives . . . life" (Job 33:4, NRSVue). All have been made from clay and filled with breath and spirit (Job 33:4).

Meditation/Journal: In general, what do animals teach you about God? Specifically, what animal teaches you best about God? Explain.

Psalm Response: "Oh! Teach us to live well [, God]. / Teach us to live wisely and well! / Surprise us with love at daybreak; / then we'll skip and dance all the day long. / And let the loveliness of our Lord, our God, rest on us, / confirming the work that we do. / Oh, yes. Affirm the work that we do!" (Ps 90:12, 14, 17, TM)

Animals Given to Nebuchadnezzar

Scripture: "In the beginning of the reign of King Zedekiah son of Josiah of Judah, this word came to Jeremiah from the LORD. Thus says the LORD of hosts, the God of Israel: This is what you shall say to your masters: It is I who by my great power and my outstretched arm have made the earth, with the . . . animals that are on the earth, and I give it to whomever I please. Now I have given all these lands into the hand of King Nebuchadnezzar of Babylon, my servant, and I have given him even the wild animals of the field to serve him." (Jer 27:1, 4–6, NRSVue)

Reflection: After King Nebuchadnezzar had invaded Jerusalem and captured King Jehoichin, who had been on Judah's throne for only three months, Nebuchadnezzar took the king and all the royal household to Babylon as captives of war in 597 BCE and establish Jehoichin's uncle, Zedekiah (597–586 BCE), as client king. As long as Zedekiah paid the tribute required of him, all was well, but when he decided to rebel, Nebuchadnezzar came back to Jerusalem, killed Zedekiah's three sons, and took Zedekiah—after blinding him—to Babylon, after he destroyed the temple in Jerusalem and the city's walls, leaving it a devastation. The prophet Jeremiah, reading the signs of the times, predicted that this was going to happen. The Scripture passage above, is the first of his predictions; what a gift it made to Zedekiah on his coronation day! The LORD tells Jeremiah, "I have even given [King Nebuchadnezzar] the wild animals" (Jer 28:14, NRSVue) in addition to all the other lands, including Judah, which was a desolation "without humans or animals" (Jer 32:43; 36:29, NRSVue), who had fled (Jer 50:3). By giving the wild animals to King Nebuchadnezzar, God transferred his sovereign power from Judah's king to Babylon's king, from Israel to Babylon. The wild animals represented God leaving the land he gave to his chosen people and moving to Babylon!

Meditation/Journal: Where might God be handing over the wild animals of one nation to another nation today? Explain.

Psalm Response: "Alongside Babylon's rivers / we sat on the banks; we cried and cried, / remembering the good old days . . . . / Alongside the quaking aspens / we stacked our unplayed harps; / That's where our captors demanded songs, / sarcastic and mocking: / 'Sing us a happy . . . song!' / Oh, how could we ever sing GOD's song / in this wasteland? / If I ever forget you, Jerusalem, / let my fingers wither and fall like leaves." (Ps 137:1–5, TM)

Animal Nature

Scripture: ". . . [T]he whole creation in its nature was fashioned anew . . . . / For land animals were transformed into water creatures, / and creatures that swim moved over to the land." (Wis 19:6a, 19, NRSVue)

Reflection: According to the author of the OT (A) book of Wisdom, at the Exodus things did not behave as they had always done; something new took place. One new thing occurred during the crossing of the Red Sea. Land animals (oxen, cattle, sheep, etc.) passing on dry ground through the waters piled on the right and the left were like sea creatures, whereas sea creatures (frogs), usually found swimming in the water, walked on dry land. God guides the author to wisdom about "the natures of animals and the tempers of wild animals" (Wis 7:20, NRSVue). Later in the book, the author reflects on the lack of intelligence of snakes, who "even as animals . . . , are not so beautiful in appearance that one would desire them" (Wis 15:19, NRSVue). The author of the Second Letter of Peter compares false prophets to "irrational animals, mere creatures of instinct, born to be caught and killed" (2 Pet 2:12, NRSVue); the author of the Letter of Jude does the same (Jude 1:10). In Paul's First Letter to the Corinthains, the apostle reflects on nature this way: "Not all flesh is alike, but there is one flesh for humans, another for animals, another for birds, and another for fish" (1 Cor 15:39, NRSV). Thus, there are multiple biblical reflections on animal nature.

Meditation/Journal: What do you think is basic (or general) animal nature?

Psalm Response: "The God of gods—it's GOD!—speaks out, shouts, 'Earth!' / welcomes the sun in the east, / farewells the disappearing sun in the west. / 'Are you listening, dear people? I'm getting ready to speak . . . . / . . . [W]hy should I want your blue-ribbon bull, / or more and more goats from your herds? / Every creature in the forest is mine, / the wild animals on all the mountains. / I know every mountain bird by name; / the scampering field mice are my friends.'" (Ps 50:1, 7a, 9–11, TM)

Talking Animals

Scripture: ". . . [A]sk the animals, and they will teach you; / the birds of the air, and they will tell you; / ask the plants of the earth and they will teach you; / and the fish of the sea will declare to you." (Job 12:7–8, NRSVue)

Reflection: The above two verses are taken from Job's third response to his friends in the first round of speeches. Job's point is that even the animals know that nothing happens without God, who is in total control of all that occurs on earth. Job's statements about asking the animals—along with the birds, plants, and fish—presume that the animals have the ability to answer. In all of biblical literature, there are only three instances of animals speaking. The first is found in the HB (OT) book of Genesis. The serpent, who is not identified as Satan or the Devil, is described as "more crafty than any other wild animal that the LORD God had made" (Gen 3:1, NRSVue). The serpent carries on a conversation with Eve (Gen 3:1–7), ultimately convincing her to eat the fruit from the tree of the knowledge of good and evil. Eve tells the serpent that God has made it clear that she and her husband have been told by God not to eat the fruit; if they do, they will die. The serpent tells her that they will not die; they will become like God, knowing good and evil. The second animal to speak in biblical literature is Balaam's donkey. The long narrative is found in the HB (OT) book of Numbers (22:1—24:25). The prophet Balaam beats the donkey he is riding, because it keeps stopping and veering off the road. Unknown to Balaam, the donkey has been attempting to avoid the angel of the Lord (God), who is standing in the road (Num 22:23). According to the narrative, after the third beating, the LORD opens the mouth of the donkey and it speaks to Balaam (Num 22:28), whose eyes are opened to see the angel of the Lord in the road (Num 22:31). The third animal recorded to speak is found in the CB (NT) book of Revelation. The narrator records that he "heard an eagle crying with a loud voice as it flew in midheaven, 'Woe, woe, woe to the inhabitants of the earth, at the blasts of the other trumpets that the three angels are about to blow!'" (Rev 8:13, NRSVue) In other words, the eagle heralds imminent disaster. Because the eagle was known for its swiftness, it conveys the severity and unavoidable nature of the coming calamities in the revelatory story. It is type of flash forward used in films and TV episodes to notify the watcher of an event that will happen later in the story; its purpose is to keep the reader reading or the viewer watching for the event to take place.

Meditation/Journal: What has been your experiences of talking animals? Explain.

Psalm Response: "I lift you high in praise, my God . . . ! / and I'll bless your name into eternity. / I bless you every day, / and keep it up from now to eternity. / Creation and creatures applaud you, GOD; / your holy people bless you. / Generous to a fault, / you lavish your favor on all creatures. (Ps 145:1–2, 10, 16, TM)

Animal Love

Scripture: "Even unreasoning animals . . . have a sympathy and parental love for their offspring." (4 Macc 14:14)

Reflection: The author of the OT (A) Fourth Book of Maccabees states that just as human parents love their children, so do animals love their offspring. The author gives two examples. First, he presents birds, which build their nests on housetops, mountaintops, treetops, chasms, and holes in trees. After their eggs hatch, they ward off intruders to protect their fledglings by flying in circles around them and screeching at them (4 Macc 14:15–17). Second, he states that bees defend their honeycombs against intruders by stinging those who approach their hives (4 Macc 14:19). Adult animals protecting their young demonstrate the love they have for their offspring. If unreasoning animals do so, reasoning humans have more responsibility to do so. However, since the author of the Fourth Book of Maccabees is reflecting on the reasoning of a mother of seven sons, who were put to death, he concludes that reasoning trumps maternal emotion (4 Macc 14:11–13).

Meditation/Journal: Today, where do you find animal love? Today, where do you find reason trumping emotion? Today, where do you find emotion trumping reason?

Psalm Response: "GOD, my God, how great you are! / You started the springs and rivers, / sent them flowing among the hills. / All the wild animals now drink their fill, / wild donkeys quench their thirst. / Along the riverbanks the birds build nests, / ravens make their voices heard. / You water the mountains from your heavenly cisterns; / earth is supplied with plenty of water. / You make grass grow for the livestock, / hay for the animals that plow the ground." (Ps 104:1b, 10–14a, TM)

Like Wild Animals

Scripture: "Who pities a snake charmer when he is bitten / or all those who go near wild animals? (Sir 12:13, NRSVue)

Reflection: To answer the question posed by the author of the OT (A) book of Sirach, no one pieties a snake charmer when he is bitten by the snake; it is a risk he takes. Likewise, those who go near wild animals risk "the fangs of wild animals and scorpions and vipers" (Sir 39:30a, NRSVue), according to Sirach. The author of the OT (A) Second Book of Maccabees uses the image of wild animals to describe how Judas Maccabeus and nine other men escaped the slaughter of King Antiochus Epiphanes by getting away "to the wilderness" and keeping himself and his companions "alive in the mountains as wild animals do," living on what grew wild (2 Macc 5:27, NRSVue). Later in the book, their time in the wilderness is described as "wandering in the mountains and caves like wild animals." (2 Macc 10:6, NRSVue). Also, in the Third Book of Maccabees the author describes the deportation of the Jews from Egypt to Alexandria as being "brought on board like wild animals, driven under the constraint of iron bonds; some were fastened by the neck to the benches of the boats; others had their feet secured by unbreakable fetters, and in addition they were confined under a solid deck, so that, with their eyes in total darkness, they would undergo treatment befitting traitors during the whole voyage" (3 Macc 4:9–10, NRSVue). The author of the OT (A) Second Book of Esdras reminds us that on the sixth day God "commanded the earth to bring forth before [himself] cattle, wild animals, and creeping things" (2 Esd 6:53, NRSVue). After observing how wild animals lived, people began to compare those who lived in the wilderness to the lifestyle of wild animals.

Meditation/Journal: What wild animals do you consider to be a threat to you? Make a list. After each wild animal listed, explain how its lifestyle threatens your way of life.

Psalm Response: "[High God's] huge outstretched arms protect you— / under them you're perfectly safe; / his arms fend off all harm. / Fear nothing—not wild wolves in the night . . . . / Even though others succumb all around, / drop like flies right and left, / no harm will even graze you. / You'll walk unharmed among lions and snakes, / and kick young lions and serpents from the path." (Ps 91:4–5a, 7, 13, TM)

Summary

Animals share existence with humans on earth; they also share spirit with humans and are animated by God's Spirit. God made a covenant with all animals to save them from the great flood, which means that they, like humans, are worthy covenant partners. Animals are present at the covenant-making ceremony at Mount Sinai (Horeb), and, like people, cannot touch the mountain. God's power and divine nature can be seen in animals who repent, who teach, who are entrusted by God to King Nebuchadnezzar of Babylon, who are transformed by God, who speak, and who love. Biblically, there are those who live like wild animals, and there are people who are treated like wild animals by others.

3

Animal Theology

. . . O Lord, / . . . all you have created / rightly gives you praise, / for through your Son . . . , / by the power and working of the Holy Spirit, / you give life to all things and make them holy . . . so that from the rising of the sun to its setting / a pure sacrifice may be offered to your name.[1]

CREATED AND REDEEMED

Creator

Scripture: ". . . [Y]ou [, O Lord,] love all things that exist / and detest none of the things that you have made, / for you would not have formed anything if you had hated it. / How would anything have endured if you had not willed it? / Or how would anything not called forth by you have been preserved? You spare all things, for they are yours, / O Lord, you who love the living." (Wis 11:24–26, NRSVue)

Reflection: The Creator, who "out of the ground . . . formed every animal of the field and every bird of the air" (Gen 2:19, NRSVue), used his "great power and . . . outstretched arm" to make "the earth with the people and animals that are on the earth" (Jer 27:5, NRSVue). As the author of the OT (A) book of Wisdom states, he loves all that exists, otherwise he would not have created it! Included in "all that exists" are living animals, whom the Creator preserves, because they are his. In other words, God freely produces

1. "Order," RM, par 108.

all that exists and keeps it in existence by sharing his being with it. God creates, according to the author of Wisdom, because he loves all that lives. Out of his love-essence, God creates numberless beings to participate in his essence. Animals are included in the divine generosity that flows out of love. By creating animals, the Creator gives himself or shares himself. Therefore, he preserves the gift, because it reflects his infinite essence, being, and love. This is what the mother of seven sons tells her youngest child: "I beg you, my child, to look at the heaven and the earth and see everything that is in them and recognize that God did not make them out of things that existed" (2 Macc 7:28).

Meditation/Journal: What have you created that reflects your essence, being, and love? Explain.

Psalm Response: "You [, GOD,] set earth on a firm foundation / so that nothing can shake it, ever. / All the wild animals now drink their fill, / wild donkeys quench their thirst. / Along the riverbanks the birds build nests, / ravens make their voices heard. / You make grass grow for the livestock, / hay for the animals that plow the ground. / Mountain goats climb about the cliffs; / badgers burrow among the rocks. / The young lions roar for their prey, / clamoring to God for their supper." (Ps 104:5, 11–12, 14, 18, 21, TM)

Lord of Life and Spirit

Scripture: "I do not know how you came into being in my womb. It was not I who gave you life and breath nor I who set in order the elements within each of you. Therefore the Creator of the world, who shaped the beginning of humankind and devised the origin of all things, in his mercy gives life and breath back to you again . . . ." (2 Macc 7:22–23, NRSVue)

Reflection: After the death of the conqueror Alexander the Great, his empire was divided among the generals in his army. Antiochus IV Epiphanies ruled what had been the kingdom of Judah. His goal was to incorporate Greek culture and a Greek way of life among the Jews, who resisted him. The author of the Second Book of Maccabees in the OT (A) narrates a story about seven brothers and their mother who refused to eat pork, unclean food (2 Macc 7:1). As each son adheres to his faith, his mother supports him and watches him die. When the youngest son is brought forward, his mother, according to the author, was filled with a noble spirit (2 Macc 7:21b), and delivered the encouraging words in the Scripture passage above in which she states that the Creator—God—is the origin of all things, including animals. The belief that God is the Lord of life and spirit is stated in another story about torture later in the same book. An elder of Jerusalem, a man named Razis, avoids the horrendous torture by falling upon his own sword. Before he died, the narrator states that he called "upon the Lord of life and spirit to give them back to him again." (2 Macc 14:46a, NRSVue). Both stories demonstrate that God alone possesses eternal life, because he alone subsists in his own being, his own life, which he shares with both people and animals through blood and breath (spirit). People and animals, who have received the breath of life (spirit) from God, never go out of existence; divine life is changed, not ended by death. And while animals are under the dominion of people, they, nevertheless, are blood-brothers and -sisters or breath-of-life (spirit) brothers and sisters with them. Those Jews, who were tortured to death, trusted that the Lord of life and spirit would keep them in life and spirit on the other side of death; that hope, as spoken by the mother, enabled them to adhere to their faith and willingly die for it.

Meditation/Journal: For what are you willing to die?

Psalm Response: "Keep me safe, O God, / I've run for dear life to you. / My choice is you, GOD, first and only. / And now I find I'm *your* choice! / Day and night I'll stick with GOD; / I've got a good thing going and I'm not letting go. / Now you've got my feet on the life path, / all radiant from the shining of your face. / Ever since you took my hand, / I'm on the right way." (Ps 16:1, 5, 8, 11, TM)

Savior of All

Scripture: "Your steadfast love O LORD, extends to the heavens, / your faithfulness is like the mighty mountains; / your judgments are like the great deep; / you save humans and animals alike, O LORD." (Ps 36:6, NRSVue)

Reflection: Biblical steadfast love, as expressed in the verse above from the HB (OT) Psalm 36, refers to the LORD's unwavering, faithful, covenant-based love for people. It refers to persistent loyalty, kindness, and commitment. Because God's love is steadfast, he saves both humans and animals. In other words, God's steadfast love permeates the cosmos. "God made the wild animals of the earth of every kind and the cattle of every kind and everything that creeps upon the ground of every kind" (Gen 1:25a, NRSVue), states the author of the HB (OT) book of Genesis, "And God saw that it was good" (Gen 1:25b , NRSVue). In the words of Job, "In his hand is the life of every living thing / and the breath of every human being." (Job 12:10, NRSVue). Thus, whatever God creates or brings into existence with the breath of life, stays in existence as spirit.

Meditation/Journal: How do you describe your existence as spirit? If you have a pet, how do you describe his or her existence as spirit?

Psalm Response: "God's love is meteoric, / his loyalty astronomic, / His purpose titanic, / his verdicts oceanic. / Yet in his largeness / nothing gets lost; / Not a man, not a mouse, / slips through the cracks. / How exquisite your love, O God! / How eager we are to run under your wings." (Ps 36:5–7, TM)

Breath

Scripture: ". . . [T]he fate of humans and the fate of animals is the same; as one dies, so dies the other. They all have the same breath, and humans have no advantage over the animals . . . . All go to one place, all are from the dust, and all turn to dust again. Who knows whether the human spirit goes upward and the spirit of animals goes downward to the earth?" (Eccl 3:19–21, NRSVue)

Reflection: The question of the Teacher from the HB (OT) book of Ecclesiastes is based on a three-storied universe. After presenting his observation that humans and animals share the same fate—mortality—the Teacher declares that they also share the same breath or spirit that God shared when he created them (Gen 3:7). Because humans and animals are equal, according to the Teacher, humans have no advantage over animals, as was usually taught, since both return to the dust from which they are made. The question, whose answer cannot be determined, asks the reader if he or she can say that the human spirit goes upward (to the heavens, where God lives) or the animal spirit goes downward (to the earth, where animals live)—and we can add to the underworld or netherworld, where the dead live. Elihu, one of the speakers in the HB (OT) book of Job, adds to this discussion, stating: "If [God] should take back his spirit to himself / and gather to himself his breath, / all flesh would perish together, / and all mortals return to dust." (Job 34:14–15, NRSVue). God chooses not to do that, because both people and animals are emissaries of something greater, namely, to share Spirit with God and to share spirit with each other, and, more importantly, to be manifestations of God's Spirit. According to the OT (A) book of Wisdom, the Lord's "immortal spirit is in all things" (Wis 12:1, NRSVue). Thus, it is only Spirit sharing spirit or spirit sharing Spirit that transcends space and time that is eternal; dust returns to dust. However, God, who is essentially Spirit, receives the spirit of people and animals, which he graciously gave them when he created them, and in him they live forever. Spirit in flesh manifests the Creator, and when the flesh dies, spirit returns to Spirit eternally.

Meditation/Journal: With what animal do you share spirit?

Psalm Response: "Hallelujah! / Praise God in his holy house of worship, / praise him under the open skies; / Praise him for his acts of power, / praise him for his magnificent greatness; / Let every living beathing creature praise GOD! / Hallelujah! (Ps 150:1–2, 6, TM)

All in All

Scripture: "[The Father's beloved Son] is the image of the invisible God, the firstborn of all creation, for in him all things in heaven and on earth were created, things visible and invisible . . . —all things have been created through him and for him. He himself is before all things, and in him all things hold together. He . . . is the beginning, the firstborn from the dead, so that he might come to have first place in everything. For in him all the fullness of God was pleased to dwell, and through him God was pleased to reconcile to himself all things, whether on earth or in heaven . . . ." (Col 1:15–17, 18b–20, NRSVue)

Reflection: The author of the second-generation Pauline letter to the Colossians in the CB (NT) has embedded a hymn in his letter, and that hymn is the Scripture text above. The Father's Son, Jesus Anointed, is presented as the cosmic agent of creation, much like Wisdom is presented in the HB (OT) book of Proverbs (8:22–31) or the OT (A) book of Sirach (24:1–22). He is also presented as the agent of redemption, reconciling or restoring all to friendship with God. The hymn declares Jesus Anointed to be the source of everything created—which includes animals—and for whom they were created. Because he is the firstborn of all creation—meaning in existence before anything else was created, and the first after creation to be raised from the dead—in him all things hold together, and, again, all things include animals. If the fullness of God was pleased to dwell in him, then the fullness of God dwells in everything in him, including animals. That is why the author of this letter can declare that there are no more distinctions: "Christ is all and in all!" (Col 3:11, NRSVue) What this means is that everything, including animals, remains alive in him, because he is alive in them, and God is alive in all.

Meditation/Journal: In what specific ways are you alive in Jesus Anointed? And in what specific ways is Jesus Anointed alive in you?

Psalm Response: "You who sit down in the High God's presence, / spend the night in Shaddai's shadow, / Say this: 'GOD, you're my refuge. / I trust in you and I'm safe!' / Yes, because GOD's your refuge, / the High God your very own home. / 'I'll give you the best of care / if you'll only get to know and trust me' [, says GOD]. 'I'll give you a long life, / give you a long drink of salvation!'" (Ps 91:1–2, 14, 16, TM)

Immanent and Transcendent

Scripture: "Thus says the Lord GOD: Are you he of whom I spoke in former days by my servants the prophets of Israel, who in those days prophesied for years that I would bring you against them? On that day, when Gog comes against the land of Israel, says the Lord GOD, my wrath shall be aroused. For in my jealousy and in my blazing wrath I declare: On that day there shall be a great shaking in the land of Israel; the fish of the sea and the birds of the air and the animals of the field and all creeping things that creep on the ground and all humans who are on the face of the earth shall quake at my presence, and the mountains shall be thrown down, and the cliffs shall fall, and every wall shall tumble to the ground. I will summon the sword against Gog in all my mountains, says the Lord GOD . . . ." (Ezek 38:17–21, NRSVue)

Reflection: Biblical scholars are not sure who Gog is in the HB (OT) book of the prophet Ezekiel, because the material in chapters thirty-eight and following may be from a later redactor of the book. Thus, some biblical scholars think Gog to be Alexander the Great, Antiochus Eupator, or someone else. Our focus here is how the above Scripture passage illustrates both the immanence and the transcendence of God. First, the author mentions transcendent God's wrath, his holy and righteous response to those who oppress his people. God's wrath is not human anger, but is a deliberate, just, and inevitable consequence of those who intend to oppress his chosen people. The transcendent divine wrath, according to the passage, will be manifest by the immanent God with an earthquake, a biblical sign of a theophany or appearance of God on earth. The great and holy God of Israel, according to Ezekiel, promises to defeat Gog—whoever he was—with "torrential rains and hailstone, fire and sulfur" (Ezek 38:22, NRSVue) as he did Pharaoh before the Exodus—in order to display his greatness and his holiness and make himself known to the nations (Ezek 38:23). In the words of the LORD in the HB (OT) book of Genesis, the God who lives on the top level of a three-storied universe (transcendent) must go down to the second-story, earth, to see what is going on (immanent) (Gen 18:21) and to remove the threat to his people. When he arrives, animals will quake—like the earth—in his divine presence. Here it is important to note that God is not a personal being, like animals and people are; he has no body. His immanence is a spiritual presence: Divine Spirit connects to spirit, intimately, penetratingly, and closely. The LORD's transcendence becomes immanent as Spirit connects to animal spirits and human spirits alike, transcending space and time. No matter the degree of consciousness or awareness, the personal, subsistent, intelligent, free God is pure Spirit, pure being, passing through all and beyond all, connecting his Spirit to spirit. Thus, animals participate in God's essence; they are beings brought into existence by the Creator, and, as such, they are an extension of God's presence (immanence), a dwelling place for God's Spirit (transcendence), and deserve to be treated with respect, as they on earth disclose the divine presence in heaven. Experiences of Spirit connecting to human spirit and of human spirit connecting to another human spirit disclose that the presence of God is found in everything that the Creator has made, that exists. It is God himself who uncovers or reveals himself to spirits. In other words, a spiritual presence can only be grasped by the spiritual. All of the created world, including animals, bears the signature of God.

Meditation/Journal: What is different in your response to God, when he is transcendent and when he is immanent?

Psalm Response: "After Israel left Egypt, . . . / Judah became holy land . . . . / Sea took one look and ran the other way; / River Jordan turned around and ran off. / The mountains turned playful and skipped like rams, / the hills frolicked like spring lambs. / Tremble, Earth! You're in the Lord's presence! / in the presence of . . . God." (Ps 114:1–4, 7, TM)

Summary

God gives life (spirit) to everything he has created, making even animals holy and temples of divine life (Spirit). Because God loves all he has created, he keeps it in existence by endowing everything with his Spirit, which gives life and is breath, a manifestation of noble Spirit; the spirit on loan during life is returned to the Creator upon death; it does not cease to exist. When Spirit is connected to spirit, faithful God is saving both people and animals alike, because God loves all he created. Animals share the same divine breath (spirit) that humans do. Thus, after death they are reunited, incorporated, in Spirit and live forever. After the appearance in history of Jesus Anointed, the author of the Letter to the Colossians claimed him to be the agent of creation, like Wisdom in the HB (OT). As the source of all creation and bearing the fullness of God, he is all and is in all; thus, everything created remains alive in him. The transcendent God becomes imminent in creation, even in animals, by making people and animals aware of his immanence with earthquakes, which make even animals quake in the divine spiritual presence. The Spirit connected to spirit in animals keeps all creation in existence, and God (Spirit) reveals himself to all spirit-possessing creation, including animals, in some degree of spiritual awareness and keeps all in existence in himself forever.

4

Animals as Pets

LAMBS

According to the providence of the Creator, many animals have a certain role to play in human existence by helping with work or providing food and clothing.[1]

Ewe Lamb

Scripture: The prophet Nathan said to King David: "There were two men in a certain city, the one rich and the other poor. The rich man had very many flocks and herds, but the poor man had nothing but one little ewe lamb that he had bought. He brought it up, and it grew up with him and with his children; it used to eat of his meager fare and drink from his cup and lie in his bosom, and it was like a daughter to him. Now there came a traveler to the rich man, and he was loath to take one of his own flock or herd to prepare for the wayfarer who had come to him, but he took the poor man's lamb and prepared that for the guest who had come to him." (2 Sam 12:1–4, NRSVue)

Reflection: According to the six-day account of creation in the HB (OT) book of Genesis, God created sea creatures and land creatures before he created humans (Gen 1:20–25). After people were created, they began to keep some animals as pets. For example, after a lamb—sheep or goat—was born,

1. "Blessing," BB, par 942.

if its mother, for some reason, could not or would not take care of it, humans rescued it, fed it, kept it warm, and turned it from livestock in a field into a pet in the house. Biblically, it is easy to deduce that animals became pets from the story Nathan the prophet told King David. The reader is not told why the poor man has an ewe-lamb pet, except because he was poor; it may have been all he could afford. Like any pet, the poor man raised it alongside his children, like many pet owners do. And like pet owners, he fed it off his table, gave it drink out of his cup, and held it in his arms, like one would hold a child, or let it sit on his lap. In other words, the ewe lamb was like a daughter to him, until his next-door neighbor decided to take it, slaughter it, and feed it to his guest. Besides the obvious pet reference in the story, the prophet Nathan is also depicting David's activity with Bathsheba. As king, David was responsible for ensuring the rights of the poor, such as Uriah, Bathsheba's husband. It is an ewe lamb, because Bathsheba was a woman. And also, the rich man who steals the poor man's ewe lamb is David, the rich king, who has stolen Uriah's wife, Bathsheba, even though he had a whole harem of wives, and had gotten her pregnant.

Meditation/Journal: In what contemporary situation do you find Nathan's story about the ewe lamb a reality today? Explain.

Psalm Response: "On your feet now—applaud GOD! / Bring a gift of laughter, / sing yourselves into his presence. / Know this: GOD is God, and God, GOD. / he made us; we didn't make him. / We're his people, his well-tended sheep. / Enter with the password: 'Thank you!' / Make yourselves at home, talking praise. / Thank him. Worship him. / For GOD is sheer beauty, / all-generous in love, / loyal always and ever." (Ps 100:1–5, TM)

DOGS

Blessed are you, O Lord, who created the animals and gave us the ability to train them to help us in our work. Blessed are you, O Lord, who for the sake of our comfort give us domestic animals as companions.[2]

Unclean Animal

Scripture: "Like a dog that returns to its vomit / is a fool who reverts to his folly." (Prov 26:11, NRSV)

2. "Blessing," BB, par 955.

Reflection: While there are no cats mentioned in biblical literature, dogs are mentioned; however, the mention is often in negative terms, like the proverb above from the HB (OT) book of Proverbs, which observes that dogs often return to their vomit, and applies that author's negative observation to a fool, who returns to folly. The above proverb is also quoted by the author of the CB (NT) Second Letter of Peter. He compares his opponents (those who have left the faith) to dogs returning to their regurgitation (2 Pet 2:22). What the reader needs to know is that a dog in Hebrew, Israelite, and Jewish culture was considered to be an unclean animal. The HB (OT) book of Leviticus states: "All [animals] that walk on their paws, among the animals that walk on all fours, are unclean . . . ; whoever touches the carcass of any of them shall be unclean until the evening, and the one who carries the carcass shall wash his clothes and be unclean until the evening; they are unclean for you" (Lev 11:27–28). Because dogs walk on their paws and do not chew the cud, they are unclean (Lev 11:26). In the CB (NT), the author of Luke's Gospel presents a unique parable about a rich man and Lazarus (Luke 16:19–31), who was covered with sores so that the "dogs would come and lick his sores" (Luke 16:21). These are not what many dog owners today would call dog kisses. Because dogs are unclean, by licking Lazarus' sores, the dogs made the poor man unclean; the fact that Lazarus ends up with Abraham is part of the irony of the story. The same idea is expressed by the Matthean Jesus, who tells his listeners: "Do not give what is holy to dogs . . ." (Matt 7:6, NRSVue). The only biblical book in which dogs are presented in a positive light is the OT (A) book of Tobit. The author mentions that "the dog came out [of the house] with [Tobias, son of Tobit] and went along with [him and Azariah—the angel Raphael in disguise]" (Tob 6:2, NRSVue). No other mention of the dog is made in the story until the end, when they return from their journey, "[a]nd the dog went along behind them" (Tob 11:4b, NRSVue).

Meditation/Journal: What are the differences between your culture and biblical culture in terms of dogs? Explain.

Psalm Response: "The revelation of GOD is whole / and pulls our lives together. / The signposts of GOD are clear / and point out the right road. / The life-maps of GOD are right, / showing the way to joy. / The directions of GOD are plain / and easy on the eyes. / GOD's reputation is twenty-four-carat gold, / with a lifetime guarantee. / The decisions of GOD are accurate / down to the nth degree. / God's Word is better than a diamond, / better than a diamond set between emeralds." (Ps 19:7–10a, TM)

Called a Dog

Scripture: "The Philistine [Goliath] came on and drew near to David, with his shield-bearer in front of him. When the Philistine looked and saw David, he disdained him, for he was only a youth, ruddy and handsome in appearance. The Philistine said to David, 'Am I a dog, that you come to me with sticks?'" (1 Sam 17:41–43a, NRSVue)

Reflection: In the famous HB (OT) account of David and Goliath, the Philistine Goliath taunts his opponent by referring to himself derogatorily as a dog, who is approached by David with his staff, while the Philistine comes fully armed; the Philistine fails to notice that David carries a sling! Later in the same book and in a similar vein, David taunts Saul after refusing to take advantage of the king in a cave. After emerging from the cave, David asks Saul, "Against whom has the king of Israel come out? Whom do you pursue? A dead dog? A single flea?" (1 Sam 24:14) David is saying that he is insignificant, and that Saul is mistaken if he thinks David is insignificant! In the Second Book of Samuel, Abner, commander of Saul's army, asks Ishbaal, Saul's son, "Am I a dog's head for Judah?" (2 Sam 3:8a, NRSVue). Like Goliath's words to David, Abner's words to Ishbaal are reproachful. Likewise, Mephibosheth, son of Jonathan, using "dead dog" as a term of self-reproach, "did obeisance [to King David] and said, 'What is your servant, that you should look upon a dead dog such as I?'" (2 Sam 9:8, NRSV) Another reproach is uttered by Abishai, brother of Joab, David's army commander, after Shimei, a relative of Saul, accuses David of murdering members of Saul's family. Abishai asks David, "Why should this dead dog [Shimei] curse my lord the king? (2 Sam 16:9a) Also, Hazael reproaches himself as a dog, indicating his low social status, when Elisha the prophet tells him that he is to be the new king of Aram (2 Kgs 8:13).

The author of the HB (OT) book of Deuteronomy specifies that one cannot "bring the fee of a prostitute or the wages of a dog into the house of the LORD . . . in payment for any vow" (Deut 23:18). In other words, monetary Temple obligations cannot be satisfied with funds collected as a result of prostitution, either female or male (dog). In the CB (NT), the author of the Book of Revelation declares dogs, defined as sorcerers and fornicators and murderers and idolaters, and practitioners of falsehood as being outside the new Jerusalem (Rev 22:15), whereas in Paul's Letter to the Philippians, the apostle advises his reader to beware of dogs, namely, those who shamelessly are full of greed (Phil 3:2). Finally, in verses not found in all ancient manuscripts, the author of the OT (A) book of Sirach records that a headstrong wife is regarded as a dog, which, as we have seen, reveals undesirable characteristics (Sir 26:25).

Meditation/Journal: In your culture, is there a similar use of dog as a derogatory or reproachment remark? Explain.

Psalm Response: "[The Israelites] did not destroy the peoples, / as the LORD had commanded them, / but they mingled with the nations / and learned to do as they did. / They served their idols, / which became a snare to them. / They sacrificed their sons and their daughters to the demons; / they poured out innocent blood, / the blood of their sons and daughters, / whom they sacrificed to the idols of Canaan, / and the land was polluted with blood. / Thus they became unclean by their acts and prostituted themselves in the doing." (Ps 106:34–39, NRSVue)

Dog Reflections

Scripture: ". . . [T]he hearts of humans are full of evil; madness is in their hearts while they live, and after that they go to the dead. But whoever is joined with all the living has hope, for a living dog is better than a dead lion." (Eccl 9:3b–4, NRSVue)

Reflection: The author of the HB (OT) book of Ecclesiastes begins with a negative view of humankind, declaring that people's hearts are full of evil madness, while they live. Then, they die. The life lived before death is full of possibilities for the pleasure and enjoyment that life offers. Those who live their lives have hope of more possibilities for pleasure and enjoyment as long as they are joined with all living things in hope. In other words, they expect and desire certain things to happen. In ancient Israel, the dog was not only unclean, but it was one of the most despised animals, while the lion was held to be king. According to Ecclesiastes, an alive, unclean dog is better than a dead lion solely on the basis of the dog being alive. Thus, an alive, unclean dog underlines the positive value of life, using, ironically, a despised and unclean animal, to demonstrate what luck it is to be alive. More irony follows. Job, who had been a prominent member of his community, discovers that he has become the butt of ridicule by those who are younger than he is. He states that he disdains even thinking about putting the fathers of those younger than he is with the dogs, who watch his sheep (Job 30:1). Basically, Job states that the fathers of the young, being like unclean dogs, would not make good shepherds. Proverbs declares: "You grab a mad dog by the ears / when you butt into a quarrel that's none of your business" (Prov 26:17, TM). In other words, meddling in others' affairs is like holding onto a mad dog by the ears; ultimately, the dog will bite you, and those in whose affairs you butt will also end up biting you!

The prophet Isaiah characterizes Israel's leaders as dogs "without sense enough to bark, / lazy dogs, dreaming in the sun— / But hungry dogs, they do know how to eat, / voracious dogs, with never enough" (Isa 56:19b–11, TM). Later, Isaiah characterizes Israel's worship of sacrificing a lamb to be like "one who breaks a dog's neck" (Isa 66:3, NRSVue). The prophet Jeremiah records that the LORD's wrath against Judah will be demonstrated by four kinds of destroyers: "the sword to kill, the dogs to drag away, and the birds of the air and the wild animals of the earth to devour and destroy" (Jer 15:3, NRSVue).

Meditation/Journal: Is a living dog better than a dead lion? Or is butting into a quarrel that doesn't concern you like grabbing a mad dog by the ears? Or are some of your leaders like lazy dogs who do not bark?

Psalm Response: ". . . [P]acks of wild dogs come at me; / thugs gang up on me. / They pin me down hand and foot, / and lock me in a cage—a bag / Of bones in a cage, stared at / by every passerby. / They take my wallet and the shirt off my back, / and then throw dice for my clothes. / You, GOD—don't put off my rescue! / Hurry and help me!" (Ps 22:16–19, TM)

Dog Food

Scripture: The LORD said to Moses: "You shall be people consecrated to me, so you shall not eat any meat that is mangled by beasts in the field; you shall throw it to the dogs." (Exod 22:31, NRSVue)

Reflection: In preparation for the ceremony of sprinkled blood, sealing the covenant between the LORD and the Israelites and making them his consecrated people, the LORD tells Moses that the clean, consecrated people are not permitted to eat any meat mangled by wild beasts that they might find; such unclean meat is to be given as food to unclean dogs. Through the prophet Ahijah, the LORD tells the first king of Israel—Jeroboam I (931–910 BCE)—that because of his propagation of idolatry, "[a]nyone belonging to Jeroboam who dies in the city the dogs shall eat, and anyone who dies in the open country the birds of the air shall eat" (1 Kgs 14:11, NRSV). Because he has caused Israel to sin, one of Jeroboam's descendants, Baasha (909–886 BCE), is told by the prophet Jehu that the word of the LORD declares: "Anyone belonging to Baasha who dies in the city the dogs shall eat, and anyone of his who dies in the field the birds of the air shall eat" (1 Kgs 16:4, NRSVue). Later in the HB (OT) First Book of Kings, the prophet Elijah delivers the word of the LORD to another of Jeroboam's descendants—Ahab (874–853 BCE)—about him and his wife, Jezebel: "The dogs shall eat Jezebel within the bounds of Jezreel. Anyone belonging to Ahab who dies in the city the dogs shall eat, and anyone of his who dies in the open country the birds of the air shall eat" (1 Kgs 21:23–24, NRSVue, 2 Kgs 9:10a). Before Elijah confronts King Ahab, the LORD instructs him to say: "Thus says the LORD: In the place where dogs licked up the blood of Naboth (whose vineyard Jezebel had secured for Ahab by having its owner, Naboth, accused of cursing God and the king), dogs will also lick up your blood." (1 Kgs 21:19b, NRSVue). The narrator of the First Book of Kings declares Elijah's prophecies fulfilled. King Ahab was mortally wounded in battle; the blood from his wound flowed into his chariot. "So the king died and was brought to Samaria . . . . They washed the chariot by the pool of Samaria; the dogs licked up his blood . . ." (1 Kgs 22:37a, 38a, NRSVue). Also, after Jehu is anointed king of Israel (841–814 BCE), he travels to Jezreel and orders Jezebel to be thrown down from a window by some eunuchs (2 Kgs 9:33a). "So they threw her down; some of her blood spattered on the wall and on the horses, which trampled on her" (2 Kgs 9:33b, NRSVue). After he sent some men to bury Jezebel, all "they found . . . of her [were] the skull and the feet and the palms of her hands" (2 Kgs 9:35). Thus was fulfilled the prophecy of Elijah that the dogs would eat Jezebel's flesh (2 Kgs 9:36–37).

Those HB (OT) stories give meaning to a similar account found in the CB (NT). While Jesus is in a house in the region of Trye, a Syrophoenician woman, a gentile, approached Jewish Jesus and asked him to heal her daughter. He responds, saying, "Let the children be fed first, for it is not fair to take the children's food and throw it to the dogs" (Mark 7:27, NRSVue). Basically, Jesus declares that the Jews (children) are healed first; it is not right to take what belongs to the Jews and throw it to the gentiles, who were often called dogs by the Jews! However, the woman, a gentile, is not put off. She challenges him, saying, "Sir, even the dogs under the table eat the children's crumbs" (Mark 7:28, NRSVue). Because of her remark, Jesus heals her daughter. The author of Matthew's Gospel copies that story from Mark and turns the Syrophoenician woman into a Canaanite woman. The Matthean Jewish Jesus declares, "I was sent only to the lost sheep of the house of Israel" (Matt 15:24, NRSVue). Then he tells her, "It is not fair to take the children's food and throw it to the dogs" (Matt 15:26, NRSVue); his remark still favors Jews over gentiles (dogs). She counters him, saying, "Yes, Lord, yet even the dogs eat the crumbs that fall from their master's table" (Matt 15:27, NRSVue). After declaring that the gentile woman has great faith, Jesus heals her daughter (Matt 15:28). Either account presents a gentile woman, called a dog by Jesus, getting what she wants from him by simply pointing out the dog food under the table.

Meditation/Journal: Who do you think is a modern Syrophoenician or Canaanite woman? What do you think about Jesus' reference to her as a dog? Explain.

Psalm Response: "My God! Rescue me from my enemies . . . . / Wake up and see for yourself! You're GOD, / GOD-of-Angel-Armies, Israel's God! / Get on the job and take care of these pagans, / don't be soft on these hard cases. / They return when the sun goes down, / They howl like coyotes, ringing the city. / Then suddenly they're all at the gate, / Snarling invective, drawn daggers in their teeth. / They think they'll never get caught. / Finish them off in fine style! / Finish them off for good! / Then all the world will see / that God rules well . . . , / everywhere that God's in charge. / They return when the sun goes down, / They howl like coyotes, ringing the city. / They scavenge for bones, / and bite the hand that feeds them." (Ps 59:1a, 4–7, 13–15, TM)

Dog Sounds

Scripture: Moses said to the Hebrews, ". . . [N]ot a dog shall growl at any of the Israelites—not at people, not at animals—so that you may know that the LORD makes a distinction between Egypt and Israel." (Exod 11:7, NRSVue)

Reflection: While biblical authors know dogs to be unclean, they do, nevertheless, reference dogs' activities from time to time; that indicates that dogs were present and numerous, and biblical authors were familiar with their ways. For example, the reference to a dog's growl in the Scripture above, is part of Moses' words preparing the Hebrews for the tenth plague: the death of the firstborn. While every firstborn of humans and animals will die, not even a dog will growl at the Hebrews. And this will show that God distinguishes between Hebrews and Egyptians, and, of course, favors Israelites (Hebrews). The author of the OT (A) book of Judith mentions the dog's growl (Jdt 11:19), while the prophet Isaiah mentions the dog's bark (Isa 56:10). In the HB (OT) book of Judges, the LORD tells Gideon to separate his troops based on those "who lap the water with their tongues, as a dog laps" and "those who kneel down to drink, putting their hands to their mouths" (Judg 7:5, NRSVue). The action of lapping water is accompanied by the sound made by those lapping. While the reader would expect that those who imitated dogs getting a drink—lapping the water—would be sent home, they are the troops the LORD will use to give the victory over the Midianites to Gideon (Judg 7:4–8). The author of the HB (OT) book of

Lamentations declares that the Babylonians "dogged our steps / so that we could not walk in our streets; / our end drew near; our days were numbered, / for our end had come" (Lam 4:18, NRSV). The verb *dogged* means to bother persistently or to continue in a determined way. It captures the activity of a dog seeking attention; the Babylonians not only sought the attention of the people of Jerusalem and Judah, but they got it repeatedly. The author of the OT (A) book of Sirach cautions his readers about with whom they choose to associate. Using the imagery of animals, he writes, "Every creature loves its like / and every person a neighbor. / All living beings associate with their own kind, / and people stick close to those like themselves" (Sir 13:16–16, NRSV). Then, in order to make his point about being cautious with associates, he asks: "What does a wolf have in common with a lamb? / No more has a sinner with the devout. / What peace is there between a hyena and a dog, / and what peace between the rich and the poor?" (Sir 13:17–18, NRSVue) The reader may be able to hear the dog growling at the hyena. Thus, as it is in the animal world, so it should be in the human world, according to Sirach; like animals choose to be with their own kind, so humans should associate with their own class.

Meditation/Journal: What sounds do you associate with your pet? What lessons for life can you learn from your pet?

Psalm Response: "Blessed be the Lord— / day after day he carries us along. / He's our Savior, our God, oh yes! / He's God-for-us, he's God-who-saves-us. / Lord GOD knows all / death's ins and outs. / What's more, he made heads roll, / split the skulls of the enemy / As he marched out of heaven . . . . / You can wade through your enemies' blood, / and your dogs taste of your enemies from your boots." (Ps 68:19–23, TM)

Summary

In the course of biblical time, some wild animals became pets, and some domesticated animals became pets. The story of the poor man's ewe lamb indicates that she was his pet. The OT (A) book of Tobit suggests that Tobias had a pet dog, who went with him on a journey. And in the CB (NT) account of Jesus calling a gentile woman a dog, she points to the dogs on the floor under the table, most likely pets. Because they were unclean, dogs were not considered to be worthy pets in the Jewish world; if a person touched a dog, he or she became unclean. That understanding was highlighted by their return to their vomit, not to mention all the other unclean things they ate. Also, because of their unclean status, it was considered to be very offensive to call a person a dog or even to reference one's self as such in an ironic, derogatory way. Even though a living dog was better than a dead lion, a dog was still unclean. Nevertheless, dogs watched sheep, bit attackers, barked, growled, and lapped water. They ate mangled beasts and human flesh and lapped human blood. Many of these latter activities further enhanced the fact that they were unclean.

5

A Theophany Named Shelbydog

. . . Lord, holy Father, almighty and eternal God, / . . . you do not cease to spur us on to possess a more abundant life . . . .[1]

1. "Appendix," Eucharistic Prayers for Reconciliation I, par 1.

RECAPITULATION

In chapter 1, we examined the biblical evidence for God creating animals of the earth, both wild and domestic, as living creatures endowed with divine life. This makes animals, who possess the breath of life, spirit bearers, even though some are classified as clean and some as unclean. No person can eat the blood of an animal, because ancient people thought that the blood signified divine life in animals; thus, blood must be given back to God, from whom it came, by pouring it into the ground.

We learned how animals share existence with humans on earth in chapter 2. Also, animals share spirit with humans, and, like humans, are animated by God's Spirit. God's power and divine nature can be seen in animals, who are presented biblically as being able to repent and to teach, and who can be transformed by God to speak and to love.

In chapter 3, we examined biblical, animal theology. God gives life (spirit) to everything he has created, making animals holy and temples of divine Spirit (life). Animals are presented as manifestations of divine Spirit; each animal's individual spirit is on loan during life and is returned to the Creator upon death, but it does not cease to exist. After Jesus Anointed appeared in history, biblical authors claimed that he was the agent of creation, and, as bearing the fullness of God, he is all and is in all; thus, everything created remains alive in him. The transcendent God becomes imminent in creation, in animals. The Spirit connected to spirit in animals and in Jesus Anointed reveals God to all spirit-possessing creation to some degree of spiritual awareness and keeps spirit in existence forever.

Biblical stories indicate that young animals became pets, as explained in chapter 4. However, the primary pets modern people possess—cats and dogs—are not presented the same way as modern people think about them. There are no house cats in biblical literature, most likely because they are associated with a god in Egyptian culture and would have been declared an idol in Hebrew, Israelite, and Jewish culture. Dogs, though present in biblical literature, are considered unclean. People kept dogs as pets, as demonstrated in the gospel account of Jesus calling a gentile woman a dog, and she responding to him by pointing out the dogs under the table. Dogs watched sheep, bit attackers, barked, growled, and lapped water. However, they also ate mangled beasts and human flesh and lapped human blood—all activities which enhanced their unclean status.

THEOPHANY

A biblical theophany is a manifestation of God. In biblical literature, the LORD (God) makes people aware of his presence—spirituality—with natural occurrences. In my book, *Divine Presence: Elements of Biblical Theophanies* (Eugene, OR: Wipf & Stock, 2017), I isolate twenty-one biblical elements that are used in biblical theophanies: mountains, sacred numbers, God's voice, people's (person's) response, cloud, water, thunder, lightning, trumpet blast, smoke, fire, earthquake, terms of the event (covenant), sign, transformation of witnesses, altar, feast, wind, light and darkness, jewels (precious stones), and dreams. When biblical authors want to indicate the presence of God, they use one or more of those elements. The response to the divine presence indicated by one or more of those elements is spirituality. Divine Spirit connects to human spirit. However, as we have seen in the previous chapters, Divine Spirit also connects to animal spirits, since animals are filled with the same Spirit as is all of creation. Thus, animals are not only bearers of Spirit, but their spirits connect to human spirit, just like human spirit connects to Divine Spirit. Awareness of divine presence in any animal form is spirituality.

I first became aware of my dog, Shelbydog, being a theophany one morning, when she was lying on a rug in the sunshine streaming through a large clear glass door on the front porch. Shelbydog was brindle in color—generally not the black and white commonly associated with dogs. Furthermore, Shelbydog's fur contained red highlights, which made her sparkle in the sunshine. As a biblical theologian, I concluded that she was manifesting to me the glory of God. That experience was two years after I had finished writing *Divine Presence*.

Applying some of the elements mentioned in *Divine Presence* to Shelbydog helped me to understand that she was, indeed, a theophany. She was very smart, and she understood most of whatever I said to her. Furthermore, even in her older years, she was able to learn new things. She was born on April 7; seven is a theophanic number referring to completion. Biblically, it is the sum of three, the number used to indicate the divine (having nothing biblically to do with Trinity), and four, the number used for the created order. The number seven is used repeatedly in biblical literature. Also, Shelbydog died on June 30; not only is three the number for the divine presence, but the number ten is contained three times in thirty; ten, or any of its multiples, signifies totality; there are over two hundred direct biblical references to ten.

While God is Spirit and has no voice, the Bible records God speaking, because God is anthropomorphized. God speaks in the language of the biblical writer. Shelbydog spoke, too. When she was happy, she squealed with delight; when she wanted to play or to go outside, she breathed heavily; when she walked by, her tail swished; her toe nails click, click, clicked on the tile floor; when getting up to stretch or immediately after lying on a rug, she often sighed. By listening to her voice, I not only knew where she was in the house, but I also knew her mood.

Shelbydog hated both cloudy and rainy days. When the sunshine was not pouring through the front door, she was restless. She would wait patiently for the sunshine to stream through the door, but when that didn't happen, she would wander around the house looking for me. She, being full of spirit, sought to connect to my spirit through presence, ear scratching, petting, or words.

Water played an important role in our relationship. Shelbydog had two aluminum bowls of water; one was in the kitchen and one was on the front porch where she spent most of her time. When we went outside for a walk, I usually carried a bottle full of water; we would stop and I would ask her if she wanted a drink. If she did, she would sit, and I would pour water into my left hand from the bottle in my right hand, and she would lap the water. After we got a dog water bottle, she would lap the water from the trough attached to the bottle. On a warm day, Shelbydog would drink all the water in one of her bowls and lots out of the other and half of the water bottle. Besides drinking, water played a role in Shelbydog's every three-week bath. Because she had been sprayed with a hose when she was a puppy, she hated getting a bath. However, we transformed that experience of water. I began talking about her bath five days before it was scheduled to take place. Then, on the morning it was to take place, I would call her to come to the bathroom shower and get her bath. Gradually, that routine eased her concerns about getting a bath. She got so comfortable with it that on days when it was to occur, she would go to the bathroom and wait for me to come and give her the bath! If on a walk we crossed a stream, Shelbydog had to get into it. For a few years at home, we had a kiddie pool. After a walk she loved to step in the stream or the pool and sit down so that the water flowed over her, while she held her head alone above the water.

Shelbydog was scared of loud thunder. When she came to live with me, she was scared of all thunder and other loud noises, like firecrackers. I eased her fear by calling her to sit in front of the front porch door with me kneeling behind her. I kept telling her, "Nothing will hurt you." This eased her fear to the point that, unless the thunder was loud, she would go sit in front of the door when it was raining and watch the rain. If loud thunder occurred, she would find me and lie at my feet. One night she heard thunder, awakened me, and wanted to go sit on the front porch in front of the door and watch the rain fall!

The response she had to lightning was like that of thunder. She would often awaken me during the night to let me know that she had seen lightning. Usually, with a few seconds, I would see it flashing behind the window shades. I would tell her, "It will not hurt you." After hearing those words, she would curl on her bed, and I would pull her blanket over her, and both of us would return to sleep.

While we never heard a trumpet blast, we did live close enough to a major street in our city where we could hear ambulance sirens, firetruck sirens, and storm sirens frequently. Because those didn't last very long, both of us would resume sleep. Only if the storm siren persisted would I arise and turn on the TV to see if we needed to do anything. Often, we heard the cannon at the college a few blocks from us; it was shot when the football team scored a goal. At first, Shelbydog was scared of it, but with time and me telling her "It will not hurt you," she felt comfortable hearing it.

Shelbydog not only liked seeing the fire in the fireplace on cold winter nights, but she was the color of fire. Her red highlights sparked me to say to her many times, "You are my burning bush."

I made a covenant with Shelbydog, after her former owner gave her to me. We were good friends, and he and his wife were moving to Florida. Because Shelbydog hated humidity, he knew that he and his wife could not take her with them. She had been spending a lot of her time with me, so I said I would keep her, and they gave her to me. I made a promise to Shelbydog that I would take care of her, as long as she lived.

After she died and was buried in a local pet cemetery, I went to her grave a few days after her burial to visit. I asked her to give me a sign that her spirit—she being a theophany—was united to her Creator. I wasn't afraid to ask for a sign, since God gives many different signs to people in the Bible. After returning home from visiting her grave, I stood outside for a few minutes and, looking up, I saw a large black bird freely wing its way overhead, and I knew that was Shelbydog's spirit; she was always a free spirit. A few days later, while taking my morning walk, I found a plastic poop bag lying on the sidewalk; it was folded in the just same way as I used to fold one of Shelbydog's and keep it attached to her leash, in case I needed a second one in addition to the first one that I kept in my pants pocket. The third sign I received was in an article I read in a spiritual magazine about the need for Animal Saints. Not only did I know that Shelbydog was a theophany, but I knew that she was a saint, because, even though her body had been buried, her spirit was united to the Spirit. Those signs fostered my own spirituality by making me even more aware of the divine presence Shelbydog bore. I concluded that she and I are eternally and spiritually inseparable from each other but also inseparable from God.

The goal of spirituality is transformation or change. Shelbydog taught me to be present to her, and my presence to her was presence to God, and her presence to me was presence to God, who was present to both of us. Shelbydog was a theophany to me. Her brindle color with red highlights, her pointed ears, black nose, big brown eyes, etc. are accidental to the spirit she was and the Divine Spirit she manifested and disclosed. I recognized this when she would come to my chapel and walk under the altar there and lie in front of it.

Shelbydog and I feasted (at meals) three times a day. Because of her chronic stomach issues, she ate when I did. She would lie on a rug by the kitchen door and watch me prepare her food: kibble, medicine wrapped in canned dog food, cut chews (Shelbydog would not chew chews; I had to cut them and put them in her bowl with her kibble), and shred small pieces of boiled chicken and place them on the top. After she cleaned her bowl, she got a small dog bone and a large dog bone. When guests were present, I would often give them a small piece of a bone to share with Shelbydog during the meal. That way I, guests, and Shelbydog shared a feast together.

Shelbydog liked the wind. She liked to go for a walk when the wind was blowing. She also liked to sit in front of the door and watch the trees bend in the wind. In the fall, she liked to watch the leaves be driven by the wind across the driveway.

Circadian rhythms were manifested in Shelbydog's response to light and darkness. When the days were longer in the spring and the summer, she arose early in the morning and went to bed later in the evening; she spent most of the day on the enclosed front porch. When the days were shorter in the autumn and winter, she slept later and went to bed earlier. Sometimes, she would go to her bed, which was located near mine, long before I went to bed, and at other times she would fall asleep on her front porch rug, and I would cover her with a blanket; later, when I'd call her to come to bed, she would arise and go to her bed.

When Shelbydog was dreaming, I'd hear her making sounds and I would awaken. Many times I awakened to see her feet moving; she was dreaming that she was running. If her sounds turned from being excited to moaning, I would lean over from my bed and gently awaken her by petting her. I'd tell her she was dreaming, pull her blanket over her, and she would be asleep again in a few minutes.

Because Shelbydog manifested so many of the elements of a theophany, I concluded that she was a theophany. As I got to know her better and to love her deeply, I became aware that I got to know God better and to love him deeply through her. Shelbydog, who was connected to her Creator (spirit-Spirit) taught me to let Spirit connect to my spirit. My awareness deepened my spirituality. Both of us were the result of the Creator desiring to be united to what he created. I can only hope that Shelbydog got to know her Creator, whom she revealed, to me.

From a Christian perspective, I also refer to Shelbydog as a silent missionary. She was a silent missionary because she preached divine presence without saying a word and converting many. Her missionary work reminded me of Psalm 19: "The heavens are telling the glory of God, / and the firmament proclaims his handiwork. / Day to day pours forth speech, / and night to night declares knowledge. / There is no speech, nor are there words; / their voice is not heard; / yet their voice goes out through all the earth, / and their words to the end of the world" (Ps 19:1–4, NRSVue). After the manager of the pet cemetery where Shelbydog was buried told me that there was usually no one there when he and his crew buried a pet, I was amazed with eleven other people (12 including me) attended her burial.

Before churches became institutions, saints were declared by ordinary people who knew extraordinary other people. Once I understood that Shelbydog was a theophany, it wasn't hard to conclude that she was a saint. She displayed unconditional love, and she communicated by sharing her toys, raising her front paw, grunting, and posturing—lying on her belly with all four feet in the air, lying by my chair, searching for me in the house, etc. Her presence transformed me, which is exactly what spirituality is supposed to do.

I like using the image presented by Paul in his Second Letter to the Corinthians. He writes about seeing the glory of God in the face of Christ. In Shelbydog I saw the glory of God. She was a treasure in a clay jar, making clear that her extraordinary power belonged to God and did not come from her or anyone else (2 Cor 4:7). In other words, she was a theophany.

Conclusion

Only God would choose to manifest himself in a biblically unclean animal: Shelbydog! While dogs enjoy a life of relative ease in contemporary cultures as pets, the biblical world shocks modern people with its words depicting dogs at the bottom of the social scale, especially when biblical words refer to dogs' diets as disgusting, devouring whatever is left over along with human corpses, not to mention human enemies being described as dogs prowling around the city. Not only do biblical characters identify themselves as dogs to draw attention to their miserable condition, but they also call others, especially gentiles, dogs in order to insult them. Given all this, I stand back in spiritual awe, when I realize that Shelbydog was a theophany, a manifestation of God in a biblically unclean creature!

For more information on Shelbydog see: *The Shelbydog Chronicles by Shelby Cole as Recorded by Mark G. Boyer: A Novel* by Mark G. Boyer (Eugene, OR: Resource Publications, 2022), *More Shelbydog Chronicles: Reflections on a Dog's Life by Her Friend, Knowing Your Pet* by Mark G. Boyer (Eugene, OR: Resource Publications, 2024), and *Final Shelbydog Chronicles: Touched by a Dog* by Mark G. Boyer (Eugene, OR: Resource Publications, 2025).

6

Animals and Saints

"... [W]ith the whole of creation, / freed from the corruption of sin and death, / may we glorify you [, O merciful Father,] through Christ our Lord, / through whom you bestow on the world all that is good."[1]

FRANCIS OF ASSISI

St. Francis of Assisi (1181–1226 CE) is well known in legend for his ability to relate to animals. In popular iconography he is usually depicted standing among trees with a bird or two perched in their branches or on his shoulders. Under the trees can be found a donkey, a sheep, a wolf, rabbits, and a duck. In statuary, Francis is found standing in bird baths with birds perched on his shoulders or on his hand. Some statues feature a fawn or wolf standing beside him along with one bird on a shoulder and one bird sitting in the palm of his hand.

1. "Order," RM, par 122.

Among other things, Francis was known for his ability to communicate with animals. While it is difficult to get behind the legends, it is possible to say that he recognized the spirit in animals, which seem to recognize the same spirit in him, and both responded to relationship accordingly. Francis' knowledge of biblical literature with its three talking animals may have made him aware of the divine presence animals can reveal. In some parts of the world, on October 4, the Memorial of St. Francis of Assisi in the Roman Catholic Church, animals are blessed.

One of the most well-known legends concerning Francis of Assisi features the wolf of Gubbio. The people and animals of the town of Gubbio were being attacked by a wolf, and they were unable to defeat the wolf. Francis intervened by meeting the wolf outside the town, calming it, and making peace by promising the starving wolf that the people of the town would provide regular food, if it would stop attacking people and animals. The wolf agreed to Francis' negotiation by placing its paw in Francis' hand, and all lived in peace. Francis' trust of and compassion toward animals are illustrated by this legend.

Another legend features Francis preaching to a flock of birds, who listened attentively, stretching their necks and flapping their wings. Francis' connection to the natural world and his understanding that spirits of animals could connect to his spirit and to the Divine Spirit implies that all creation is connected.

A follower of Francis gave him a pet lamb, but he could not keep it because of his vow of poverty. He gave the lamb to a woman, who cherished his gift so much that she made him clothes from the lamb's wool. Francis was the first to erect a living nativity scene at Christmas complete with an ox and a donkey in a cave in the town of Greccio.

Another legend concerns a trapped rabbit. While Francis was in Greccio, a friar brought him a live, wild rabbit that had been caught in a trap. Francis took the rabbit, scolded it for getting into the trap, and released it. But the rabbit did not run away; it hopped onto Francis' lap for safety. He stroked it, and he tried to release it again, but it came back to him. Finally, he gave it to a friar to take to the woods and release it there. This legend illustrates Francis' understanding that all animals were brothers and sisters to humankind and deserving of respect as an expression of God's Spirit.

OTHER LEGENDS FEATURING ANIMALS AND SAINTS

A Wolf and Abba Macarius

"... [When] Abba Macarius the Great [, a desert father (300–391 CE),] ... was working the harvest with ... brothers, a wolf opened its mouth and let out a great cry, its eyes staring up to heaven to the Lord. The saint stopped and smiled with tears in his eyes."

"When the brothers saw him, they were amazed. They threw themselves down at his feet, entreating him 'We beg you, our father, tell us why you were staring with tears in your eyes.'"

"While he stared with tears in his eyes, his face shone like fire, like the rays of the sun, on account of the grace of our Lord Jesus Christ that was in him. He said to them, 'Didn't you hear what this wolf cried out?'"

"They said to him, 'He cried up to the lover of humanity, to the compassionate one alone, who possessed the treasuries of numerous mercies, our Lord Jesus Christ, saying, "If you're not going to care about me and provide me with my food, at least tell me why I'm suffering. You were the one who created me." If even flesh-eating beasts have understanding and cry up to the goodness of our Lord Jesus Christ and he nourishes all of them, then how will he not care about us who are rational beings, with his bountiful mercy and compassion?'"

"As the luminary and light-giver was saying these things to the brothers, the wolf stood with its mouth agape Afterwards, the beast went to the place where God had prepared food for it, and all the brothers prostrated themselves and venerated the holy feet of our righteous father, the Spirit-bearer Abba Macarius the Great, giving glory to our Lord Jesus Christ."[2]

The Lion and Jerome

While St. Jerome was living as a desert hermit, an injured lion came to him with a thorn in its paw. While other hermits ran away in terror, Jerome calmly approached the lion, removed the painful thorn, and the lion became Jerome's faithful companion and pet. The lion lived with Jerome for many years, and was particularly known for guarding his donkey.

2. Vivian, *Fire*, 378–9.

Otters and Cuthbert

St. Cuthbert, a seventh-century Celtic monk and saint, often went to the coast of northern England to pray. A fellow monk followed him and watched him enter the cold sea and pray all night. In the morning, he returned to shore, and the otters emerged from the water and warmed his feet with their fur.

The Dog and Roch

According to the legend, after St. Roch tirelessly cared for Italian plague victims, he contracted the disease and retreated to a nearby forest to die alone. However, a dog from a nearby village began to bring him bread to eat; the dog also licked his infected sores. One day, the dog's master, a nobleman, followed the dog and discovered St. Roch; the nobleman helped to nurse Roch back to health.

The Blackbird and Kevin

The Irish hermit St. Kevin was deep in prayer in a cave. He extended his hand, and a blackbird flew upon it and built a nest in the palm of his hand. To avoid disturbing the bird and the eggs it placed in the nest in Kevin's hand, he remained perfectly still, like a statue, for the weeks it took for the eggs to hatch and the fledglings to grow old enough to fly away. The legend emphasizes Kevin's patience and harmony with nature.

The Hare and Melangell

The Welsh legend of St. Melangell, a hermitess, begins with Prince Brochwel of Powys' hounds chasing a hare, who took refuge in Melangell's robe. The dogs refused to harm the hare, and the prince's hunting horn mysteriously was unable to sound. Impressed by St. Melangell's piety, the prince granted her land to establish a religious community of women. He also ensured her that no wild animals would ever be hunted there again.

Animals and St. Martin de Pores

St. Martin de Pores was a Dominican lay brother, who was known for his love and care for all animals. One legend recounts how he convinced a stray dog, a cat, and a mouse, who were causing problems in a monastery, to eat from the same bowl in peace. Another legend records his care for a colony of mice, with whom he negotiated a truce; they could stay in his room as long as they did no damage.

The Piglet and Anthony

A wild sow had a piglet who was blind. St. Anthony, a desert hermit, cured the blind piglet. Then, the sow followed him and served as his faithful guardian.

The Bear and Seraphim

There is a legend about a bear visiting the hermitage of the Russian Orthodox St. Seraphim, who spend a lot of time in the forest. The wild bear would visit him, and Seraphim would feed it by hand. The bear was gentle and obedient to him.

The Water Beast and Columba

The water beast, at first called a monster in the River Ness, ultimately became the legend of the Loch Ness Monster. St. Columba, a sixth-century Irish monk, encountered it. After he saw it attack a man, he commanded it to retreat, and it did.

The Raven(s) and Benedict and Meinrad

When an enemy attempted to poison St. Benedict with a loaf of bread, he instructed a raven, whom he regularly fed, to take the poisoned bread and fly away with it. The bird did as he was instructed. Ravens, whom St. Meinrad regularly fed at his hermitage in the mountains, followed the robbers, who had killed him, into the closest town to let the people know that St. Meinrad was dead.

The Dog and John Bosco

A dog named Gray appeared at times of danger to protect the nineteenth-century St. John Bosco. To attackers, the dog was savage, but to John Bosco he was gentle.

The wolf and Austreberthe

While this legend is similar to that of the wolf of Gubbio and St. Francis of Assisi, it features a wolf, who killed a donkey. The abbess, St. Austreberthe, is reported to have commanded the wolf to make amends by carrying the laundry for the nuns in the donkey's place, and he did so for the rest of his life.

WHISPERERS

While legends are legends, they nevertheless recall and illustrate how various people have connected their spirit to various animal spirits and, in so doing, to connect to the Spirit. Today we refer to such people as whisperers. An animal whisper is a person who communicates with animals—horses, dogs, cats, etc. A whisperer claims to possess an innate, intuitive ability to communicate with animals by understanding their thoughts, feelings, and needs through cues, body language, and empathetic connections. From a biblical perspective, whisperers are those who make a connection with their spirit to the animal's spirit, and, by doing so, connect to the Divine Spirit. The whisperer senses the animal's internal state, and with a deeper awareness or feeling knows the animal's perspective. It may be telepathic communication, mind-to-mind messaging, or it may be empathy, a sensory understanding of an animal's self and world. Some whisperers help veterinarians diagnose medical issues for pets, while others help resolve behavioral problems. Like saints and animals of the past, modern whisperers even work with wild animals to work together communication and understanding to facilitate peaceful coexistence with people. Animal whisperers claim a special connection to animals that transcends typical understanding in the same way that some biblical writers recognized both the spirit-spirit connection and the spirit-Spirit connection.

Bibliography

"Appendix to the Order of Mass: Eucharistic Prayers for Reconciliation I." In *The Roman Missal: Study Edition*, 757–64. Collegeville, MN: Liturgical, 2110.

Book of Blessings. New York, NY: Catholic Book, 1989.

"Order for the Blessing of Animals." In *Book of Blessings*, 409–16. New York, NY: Catholic Book, 1989.

"The Order of Mass." In *The Roman Missal: Study Edition*, 511–673. Collegeville, MN: Liturgical, 2112.

Piault, Bernard. *What is the Trinity?* New York, NY: Hawthorn, 1959.

The Roman Missal: Study Edition. Collegeville, MN: Liturgical, 2012.

Shapiro, Rami. "Thriving in Uncertainty: Cultivate Gratitude for our Interdependence." *Spirituality and Health: A Unity Publication* 2:5 (2025) 32–4.

Vivian, Tim. *Becoming Fire*. Collegeville, MN: Cistercian Publications, 2024.

Recent Books by Mark G. Boyer
Published by Wipf & Stock

Nature Spirituality: Praying with Wind, Water, Earth, Fire

A Spirituality of Ageing

Weekday Saints: Reflections on Their Scriptures

Human Wholeness: A Spirituality of Relationship

A Simple Systematic Mariology

Praying Your Way through Luke's Gospel and the Acts of the Apostles

An Abecedarian of Animal Spirit Guides: Spiritual Growth through Reflections on Creatures

Overcome with Paschal Joy: Chanting through Lent and Easter—Daily Reflections with Familiar Hymns

Taking Leave of Your Home: Moving in the Peace of Christ

An Abecedarian of Sacred Trees: Spiritual Growth through Reflections on Woody Plants

Divine Presence: Elements of Biblical Theophanies

Fruit of the Vine: A Biblical Spirituality of Wine

Names for Jesus: Reflections for Advent and Christmas

Talk to God and Listen to the Casual Reply: Experiencing the Spirituality of John Denver

Christ Our Passover Has Been Sacrificed: A Guide through Paschal Mystery Spirituality—Mystical Theology in The Roman Missal

Rosary Primer: The Prayers, The Mysteries, and the New Testament

From Contemplation to Action: The Spiritual Process of Divine Discernment Using Elijah and Elisha as Models

Love Addict

All Things Mary: Honoring the Mother of God—An Anthology of Marian Reflections

Shhh! The Sound of Sheer Silence: A Biblical Spirituality that Transforms

What is Born of the Spirit is Spirit: A Biblical Spirituality of Spirit

Very Short Reflections—for Advent and Christmas, Lent and Easter, Ordinary Time, and Saints—through the Liturgical Year

Living Parables: Today's Versions

My Life of Ministry, Writing, Teaching, and Traveling: The Autobiography of an Old Mines Missionary

300 Years of the French in Old Mines: A Narrative History of the Oldest Village in Missouri

Journey into God: Spiritual Reflections for Travelers

Monthly Entries for the Spiritual but not Religious through the Year: Texts, Reflections, Journal/Meditations, and Prayers for the Spiritual but not Religious

The Shelbydog Chronicles by Shelby Cole as Recorded by Mark G. Boyer: A Novel

Four Catholic Pioneers in Missouri: Lamarque, Kenrick, Fox, and Hogan: Irish Missionaries and Their Supporter

Smothered with Inexhaustible Mercy: An Anthology of Poems

Spirituality for the Solitary: A Handbook for Those Who Live Alone

Seasons of Biblical Spirituality: Spring, Summer, Autumn, Winter

Biblical Names for God: An Abecedarian Anthology of Spiritual Reflections for Anytime

More Shelbydog Chronicles: Reflections on a Dog's Life by Her Friend, Knowing Your Pet

His Mercy Endures Forever: Biblical Reflections on Divine Mercy for Anytime

The Roman Catholic Lectionary and the Bible: Analysis, Conclusions, Suggested Alternatives

The Spirit of the Lord God: Biblical Names and Images for the Holy Spirit; An Abecedarian Anthology of Spiritual Reflections for Anytime

A Biblical Morning & Evening Prayer Manual: A Modern Book of Hours, Ways to Begin and End the Day

The Folks in the Woods: A Memoir of Brown Hollow, Missouri, 1874–1991

The Liturgical Environment: What the Documents Say about Roman Catholic Churches, Fourth Edition, Updated and Revised

Eavesdropping on Paul: Reading Others' Biblical Mail

Biblical Creation Stories: Plural Ways to Nourish Spirituality

Living with Grace: John Denver Spirituality in Song and Word: An Abecedarian of Themes

Spiritual Oxygen: Biblical Spirituality for the 21st Century

Final Shelbydog Chronicles: Touched by a Dog

Biblical Prophets from A to Z: Known and Unknown

Visit Wipf and Stock, https: //wipfandstock.com, for books by this author.

www.ingramcontent.com/pod-product-compliance
Lightning Source LLC
LaVergne TN
LVHW020656100826
845148LV00012B/2513

* 9 7 9 8 3 8 5 2 6 9 7 4 7 *